A Single Parent's Guide to Raising Children God's Way

Winsome Tennant

A Single Parent's Guide to Raising Children-God's Way

Dedications

I would like to dedicate this book to My Lord and Savior without whom this project would not be possible. I cried out to Him for a dream and He lovingly gave one to me. Never in my wildest imaginations would I have thought I could do something like this. I am a believer that nothing that happens in our life ever goes unnoticed by Him. He has taken my life as a single parent and turned it into a book. Who would have thought this possible but Him.

To my daughter, my beautiful angel friend and confidant. You have been my inspiration. Without you I would not have a story to tell. You have been my staunchest supporter. You saw something in the dream that I didn't. You would walk in bookstores and envision the book. You have encouraged me every step of the way. I remember the Sunday afternoon you took me to Barnes & Noble and told me to walk around and envision my book as a best seller. Your life is an example to young women all over the world. You have shown by your lifestyle and conduct that you can live clean in a dirty world. Your love for the Lord inspires young and old alike. I pray you will continue to walk in God's favor and blessing. You are one of the things I did right in my life and I love you more than my words can say.

My Pastor: Your faithful teaching of God's Word has been a great source of help and inspiration. Thank you for living a life that shows us how to walk out our faith and dream big.

Barbara Nagle, my friend. God has truly blessed me. You were one of the first people I met in the states and after 25 years of friendship, you still love me. You were there when the fire department told me I had to leave my apartment because of carbon monoxide during my pregnancy. You were there when I called to ask if you had prune juice, you said no but ten minutes later you were at my door holding the bottle. You were there when I was told by the hospital that I could not take my baby home without a car seat, you showed up with one. You were there when my kitty died and no one else understood why I was crying so hard. You have always been there financially as well. No one knows or even understands the depth of our friendship, but God does and I thank Him often for you

Foreword

W insome Tennant was born and raised in the heart of
Jamaica, West Indies, and led a pretty rough life after
the death of her father. Her mother had moved to Europe
when Winsome was only four years old and did not return
after the death of her father. So the task of raising Winsome
and her siblings was left up to relatives to decide who would
take on the responsibilities of five children left orphaned
by the untimely death of their father. The lot as they say
fell to her aunt, and 10-year old Winsome was forced to
grow up fast as the responsibilities of house work under the
abusive dictatorship of her aunt, the new guardian, piled
high. Though not the youngest of her siblings, Winsome
was nevertheless the most depended upon to handle the less
than desirable circumstances she and her family had been
put under. Though raised under the law of religion, no make-
up, jewelry, pants or perms for women etc-Winsome did not
truly know the Lord until she became a teenager and met
Him for herself. She was being abused by her aunt, physi-
cally, psychologically and emotionally, and her Heavenly
Father was her sole support and comfort during these harsh
adolescent and early adult years. But God had equipped her
for this life. She was always very strong, outspoken, and

bold in her mannerisms, and for this reason she was feared by some and disliked by others. God began to reveal Himself to her and show her visions and give her dreams about situations around her. She could tell people of scenarios she had never witnessed through the revelation of the Holy Spirit, and many dangerous situations were avoided this way—God was preparing her.

At 22, Winsome moved to the United States with her younger brother and prepared to begin her life in a new place, finally free from all of the negativity she had been raised around. She was free...so free in fact, that she backslid and began to live her life without God and the restrictions of the religiosity she was raised under. During this season, she met a man that at the time seemed to be the one for her. Their relationship reached new heights, and, after finding out that she couldn't have children, a determined Winsome became sexually active, and surprisingly became pregnant. Doctors stood in amazement. Meanwhile, Winsome's boyfriend decided that he wanted nothing to do with raising a child, and left her, later signing away his rights to his daughter.

At 28, a single mother, and not serving the Lord, Winsome had reached a crossroads. Her family was of little support, and though her mother now also lived in New Jersey, that relationship had been estranged. She had nowhere else to look but up, and God met her where she was. Having grown up with nothing but abuse, discouragement and frustration, and loosing her father to a brain tumor, and her mother's reluctance to come home after the death of her father, Winsome had little idea of how life would turn out. This was not the ideal example to follow in raising a child. What did she know of guidance and affection? What did she know of telling a baby girl that she loved her? And in the years to come, how would she know how to be supportive, sensitive and encouraging? These were concepts completely missing from her childhood memories. She had to give the child to

Jesus and pray that He would guide her through the process of motherhood. As always, He proved faithful.

When my mother told me that God had instructed her to write this book, I was thrilled. Growing up as an only child of a single mother has definitely not been easy, but I wouldn't trade the *way* I was raised for the most perfect family in the world. My mother truly leaned on the Lord for everything that concerned me. I remember waking up early mornings seeing her hovering over me in prayer, just covering me in the blood of Jesus. She never ceased to counsel me and use life experiences to show me the importance of walking with the Lord and living each day for Him. Now, at 20 years old, I can say that God the Father is truly everything to me and I plan on raising my kids God's way, just like my Mommy did with me. I will seek God's face for every decision concerning my family and myself. I will endeavor to bring Him pleasure in all I say and do. But this determination to live for God did not come automatically, it came through the diligent prayers of my mother and my following the example she gave me before I even knew how to pray. What a legacy! I pray that you read this book with open hearts and minds. I assure you that every story is true, every scripture time-tested, and every experience real. Prepare for the journey of a lifetime, parents. You have been given such a special and beautiful task--raising a godly child. Whether you're going it alone like my mother, or if you have a husband or wife at your side, God is still the best parent in the world. Don't leave Him out. Invite Him into your family and watch Him at His best as He helps you to raise *His* children *His* way.

Sheridan J. Tennant

INTRODUCTION:
THE PROPHETIC DREAM

*ON THE MORNING OF JANUARY 26, 2003 AT ABOUT
4:46 AM I AWAKENED FROM A DREAM, IT WENT AS
FOLLOWS:*

I dreamt that we were having a conference at my church, Faith Fellowship Ministries World Outreach Center. My pastor and guest speaker were walking down the aisle ministering to people. When they got to me, the visiting minister stopped and exclaimed, "Oh my gosh! It is you! I have read your books and they are *good*." As I was leaving the sanctuary, I said to someone, "She spoke prophetically into my future; this is the third person that has told this to me. I am supposed to be writing books to help families raise their children." After the service, a sister in the Lord came up to me and said, "I knew that you would get a word." I responded jokingly, "You did not." Then I thought to myself that I should have bought the tape. Immediately, my brother came up to me and handed it to me saying, "I had to return the ten tapes I originally bought so that I could get you yours." The title of the tape series he gave me was <u>Four Principles To The Will of God</u>.

When I awoke I said to myself *this is only a dream*. Then I heard the Holy Spirit respond, "Though the vision tarry wait for it, it will surely come, it will not tarry." I knew the scripture reference so I got up and marked it in my bible (Habakkuk 2:3).

Before I had this dream, I had been praying for the Lord to give me a dream that I could call my own. For, you see, I had no dream or plans for my future. I had dedicated the past 19 years to raising my daughter for Him, and had made no plans for what I would do when she left for college. I had been asking the Lord to teach me how to dream, give me a goal. On January 6, 2003 at 11:06 a.m. while sitting at my desk at work, the Holy Spirit said to me, "I am the Lord your God; walk before me and be blameless, and I will make my covenant between me and you, and will multiply you exceedingly." I knew the words sounded familiar so I opened my bible and turned right to it (Genesis 17:1-2).

I said to the Lord, "I can't be perfect, you've seen the times I have messed up." He responded, "Neither was Abraham." The aforementioned dream came about three weeks later.

I had no idea what God wanted me to write. There were times when I could hear the words and I would write things down, but I had no idea what it took to write a book, let alone *books*. I decided to sit at my computer and write down the things that He had given me, and continued to reveal to me. I knew that in His timing He would bring it all together. After all, it was His dream and His books. I simply gave the dream back to Him, so that He could bring it to pass, and He is doing just that.

IN THE BEGINNING GOD

My prayer is that this book will be a practical tool and guide in helping single parents who are going it alone, either by choice, divorce or widowhood. The best time to start any training is at the beginning. What I mean is, start in the womb, or as soon as possible thereafter. We used to say in Jamaica, 'Bend the tree while it is young, because when the trunk gets hard you will have to chop it down.' The same is true of children. Training begins when they are young and impressionable. The things we take for granted, and allow to go uncorrected with our children will be the very things that will cause a problem later on in their development.

The key to raising Godly children begins with us as parents. We will have to develop a sensitive ear and heart to God about the children that He has so lovingly given to us. How willing are you to let God teach you something that you know nothing about? That is the key to good parenting (See James 1:5). When I became pregnant with my daughter, I was a backslider. I was told that I could not have any children, and I set out to prove the doctors wrong. I was dating her father at the time and told him that the doctors weren't sure that I could become pregnant, and that if he did not want to be the father, that he should discontinue the relationship. He was in agreement with my decision and we discussed it often. I guess in his heart he was hoping the doctors were right and he could just come along for the ride. As you will find out later, as soon as I became pregnant he began to stay away. It took 2 years, but I did become pregnant. I had a high risk pregnancy due to endometriosis and a low lying placenta that caused a lot of excessive bleeding. My family was told that they should not encourage any conversation about the baby, because there was a possibility that I would not have her. I was put on bed rest the first 10 weeks of the pregnancy, and then again at the beginning of my fifth month until she was born. I was not aware of this, so I kept talking about my baby. I would be remiss if I did not tell of the Lord's provision during this 8 month period from work. I had just started my job in February of 1984, when I became pregnant in July of that same year. I had only a few days accumulated for sick time, and here I was off on an extended leave. I cannot explain how it was all done, but it seemed that my time was miraculously extended. I was paid my full pay for a while and then disability of $126.00 per week.

I had my rent, car payment, car insurance, utilities etc. When the good Lord says He is married to the backslider He is not joking- He means every word of it. When I found out that I had to be home for the duration of the pregnancy, I had no idea how I was going to make it.

My pastor was the only one in the church I was attending at the time that knew what was going on with me. When I found out that I had to be on bed rest, I reached out to him. It was then that he asked if I would allow him to tell the congregation of my situation. I gave my permission and God in His mercy intervened on my behalf. They just about adopted me. Unbeknownst to me, they set up a schedule of who would cook, do laundry, clean my house, go shopping for me, and take me to my doctor's appointments. No one asked any questions but simply pitched in until the day my baby was born. When the money ran out, they saw to the bills, and continued to bring my groceries. WHAT A GOD! I was home for 8 months and during that time God used total strangers to meet my needs. These people were not my family, or the family of my daughter's father. They planned a shower, bought and made wonderful gifts for the baby and asked for nothing in return.

Sheridan and I remained in that church until she was just about three years of age. Then the Lord directed us to our church home, which was in Edison at the time, but is currently now in Sayreville, New Jersey. I remember after I had given my life back to the Lord, I enquired of his faithfulness to me at that time in my life. He lovingly told me that over the years, I had cast my bread on the waters, and that He had caused it to come back in my time of need through the hands of strangers (See Ecclesiastics 11:1). One morning during my time of worship, God unveiled to me the source of my castings. He said to me, "From ages thirteen through nineteen, you cleaned other people's houses, washed their clothes, took care of their babies and cooked their meals." This was true, I had done this until, at age nineteen, I made this declaration, " I will not be going to anyone's home to take care of their babies, because when I have my own, not one of them will be around to help me!" God saw all of this as having cast my bread. He remembered what I forgot. Single parents, especially single moms, He will never forsake us. I recently heard a minister say, "Do you sometimes wonder if the mistakes you make in life were somehow orchestrated by God?" Like Joseph, what the enemy had meant for evil in my life, the eleven years of abuse and free maid service, God had turned it around for my good, and today, His glory.

Well, Sheridan Jenice Tennant, was born on May 4, 1985, weighing in at 8 pounds, 21 and one-half inches long. Even after all this, I was still a dog in her vomit and a pig in her wallow. (2 Peter 2:22) But I was mindful of my Father. I never stopped going to church. I went back to full time employment when my daughter was 3 months old. This was the hardest thing I had ever done; I was sure I would miss all of her firsts. But God remained faithful. He allowed me to see her sit up for the first time at 6months, at eight months I saw her stand up for the first time, I saw her crawl, walk, and heard her first words. No one had to tell me, He allowed me to see it first. When Sheri was twelve months old, she would come to me and say, "Jesus says to tell you..." and she would give me messages and toddle back to her room. This happened quite a bit, and scared the mess out of me. I still cannot recall what she told me, but it was scary. I know most of you are saying, "Twelve-month-old babies do not have a vocabulary," but my daughter spoke her first full sentence at 9 months. Whatever God had in mind for her, He was on an accelerated course, because there is not a moment that I do not remember my daughter trying to express herself.

When Sheridan was 30 months, on a Saturday night, God got my attention. He spoke to me and said, "Get your life together, because I have plans for the child." I immediately got on my knees, cried out to Him in repentance, committed my life to Him, gave Sheri completely over to His plans and asked Him to make her His chosen, and to use her for His glory. I heard, "Many are called but few are chosen" to which I responded, "MAKE HER YOUR CHOSEN!" The rest, as they say, is history. From that time, November 1987, began a fascinating journey of obedience and commitment to God's plan for both of our lives. One of the things I requested of the Lord was that He reveal to me what He was doing, as well as what He wanted me to do so that I would not interfere with His plans for Sheridan. He has been faithful to do just that as you will see as I go along.

I was at the time attending First Baptist Church of Montclair. The word was not a challenge for me. I started to fast and pray for my pastor, and now Sheri's Godfather, to have an encounter with the Lord. He went away for a 6-month sabbatical and came back a new person. He began to really teach the word, but the people were not receptive at all. I was being blessed while others were disgruntled. He was moving away and I knew I had to find another church. I remembered someone inviting me to a big church in Edison, New Jersey, so I decided to call my friend and go for a visit. That was February of 1989, I was hooked and filled out membership information that same day. That was the turning point for both Sheri and me.

In order for you to understand where I am going with this, I must first allow you to peek into our lives. God can change our hearts, as well as our pasts. In order for us to achieve God's ultimate purpose, we must also be willing to change some things. Our past can cause us to go, as they say, "from the frying pan to the fire." Allow me to now explain how my single-parent state came about. When I was pregnant with Sheridan, her father decided to change his position about us. That is called reality and responsibility. I have always been very independent and strong willed, so when he decided to act like a fool, I made a decision to go it alone. I was told by well-meaning family members to wait until after Sheri was born, to which I responded, "Everyone knows I did not get pregnant on my own, so it doesn't matter when I end the relationship." Looking back, it was all a part of His plan. Had I continued in the relationship, I would not have raised the Godly child I have today. Single parents: do not be afraid to walk away. God is the greatest Father your children will ever have, and certainly the best HUSBAND or WIFE you will ever need. It was not always easy, but it is well worth it to trust God in all situations, and I would not change a thing. I have often told my daughter that had I done it God's way, she would have had a father. But I have introduced her to the Father of all fathers.

My father died when I was ten years old, I had not known my mother but for the first 4 years of my life, and when my father passed, my siblings and I went to live with my aunt and her family. There I experienced physical, mental, verbal and emotional abuse, mixed with religion. We were, to the church world, the happy family. We had a singing family group, my aunt was known as an evangelist and her husband a pillar of the church. We would awake early mornings to have family devotions, which was where my relationship with the Lord began at the age of thirteen. I turned to God with all of my heart during the eleven years of abuse that I suffered and He became my closest friend. When my father died, they buried the only person that ever told me he loved me. For eleven years neither my aunt nor her husband ever affirmed their love for me. I was the little maid to whoever needed my help at the time. I did not know how to receive or give love, and trusting people became very difficult for me. It would take a whole chapter to tell what my experiences were, but I'll save that for another time.

When I had my baby, God had to place His love in my heart for her. While she was an infant I had no problem loving and communicating with her, but as soon as she was able to communicate with me, I suddenly did not know what to do. I started to withdraw from my daughter. I did not know how to play with her; I never told her I loved her. When Sheri was three she asked me, "Mommy, why am I the only one who says I love you?" I had never noticed that I wasn't, because whenever she said it I would say it back. The Lord was trying to get my attention through my daughter so that I would not do to her what was done to me. Remember I told you that the Lord told me to get my life together, because He had plans for the child? Well this is where everything started to move along.

So, in conclusion to this introduction, before you continue into the subsequent chapters, I ask that you prepare to open your hearts and minds as parents of God's precious and predestined gifts. I am sure you have gathered by my introduction that I am speaking to you from the viewpoint of a woman, and a mother, whose foundation rests on faith. I will speak often of hearing God's voice, heeding God's instruction, and will reference many scriptures throughout these chapters. If you are reading these words and are not sure of where you stand with the Lord, and you would like to know more about this relationship and commitment that far exceeds the love of any man or woman, please take the time to repeat this simple prayer before you continue:

Heavenly Father,

I know that I have sinned and fallen short of your glory. At this time, I ask you to come into my life. Remove everything in me that hurts you. Relieve me of the pain and bad memories from my past. I acknowledge that your son Jesus came to Earth, was crucified for my sins, and was raised from the dead and now sits at your right hand in Heaven. Come into my heart and forgive me of my sins. Help me to realize that I am yours, and no longer a slave to sin and past mistakes. Make me the parent and individual you have predestined me to be. Help me to live for you, and to raise my child Your way.

In Jesus' name I pray, Amen

So, without further ado, I welcome you to begin this journey with me through the experiences, lessons, and nuggets of wisdom that the Lord has given me to share with you, one single parent to another, about what it truly means to raise your child God's way.

Winsome Tennant

CHAPTER ONE

THE HOLY SPIRIT MY COACH, MY TEACHER

My daughter loved to snuggle and hug- I did not enjoy it at all. She would get really close to me and I would cringe. Then I would hear the Holy Spirit say, "Hug her now." I would just about die on the inside, but I would obey. My little bundle would melt in my arms and I could not wait for her to let go. Then He would say, "Tell her you love her," another hard thing to do. It was not that I did not love my daughter I just did not know how to express it. I did not want to say it, but I did. This exercise would continue for years, until I started to hug her and say I love you without my Coach. I dreaded playing! How do I play with her? I would play hide and seek, and hide so well she would go into hysterics and then I would surface to say I would not play with her again. It breaks my heart to write this, but it will help someone. The Lord continued to do His healing work in me, and protected my daughter from emotional trauma. She once told my brother, (she was 4 at the time) "Mommy is boring." My brother said to me, "Why won't you play with your child?" I responded that I didn't know how to play with her. I did everything parents did: I took her to the park, bought her bike to teach her to ride, took her to swimming lessons, ice-skating classes, gymnastics etc. I just didn't play with her. The one thing I did was teach her by example how to pray and trust the Word of God. She learned at my knees. By the time Sheri was three, she was praying like an adult with just as much conviction. We finally got the love and touch thing down, I thought, until she began to ask to be tucked into bed. She was insistent about it, and I know now that it was God. When I would go to her room to tuck her in, she would be so happy. She even told me the other day when I was apologizing for not being a mushy mom that she only asked to be tucked in because when she slept at her friend's home, her mom did it for her. Whew! What a relief she was not traumatized!

PREPARING FOR PUBLIC SCHOOL

Get God in on it

Before Sheridan started attending Pre-K in the township where we lived, we had what were called magnet schools. As parents, we were given the opportunity to visit an open house of each school and make a decision for which school was best suited to our children. I visited the pre-k program for each school and was particularly impressed with one teacher. I left there that night and prayed that Sheri would have this woman as her teacher. I felt that she would be a wonderful mentor for the first two years of Sheridan's scholastic life. I honestly do not know what endeared her to me, but I had a sense that Sheridan would not be hindered in any way being with this teacher. I asked the Lord to make this possible, and that if she was not His choice for her, that He would show me, but I was confident He had chosen her as well.

While we were going through the summer months, getting prepared for school, I was told by someone who knew the teacher that she had been transferred to the first grade. I went back to the Lord and my prayer went something like this: *Father, you know that this was the only school and teacher that I really thought would be best for Sheridan's first years of school. If you had also chosen her, then I am asking you to have her moved back to Pre-k. I have not selected a second choice school or teacher, so please move her back so that Sheri can have her as her teacher.* I was told later that two days before school was supposed to start, the teacher was transferred back to Pre-k. She was quite upset, but the individual told her that a parent had prayed her back to Pre-kindergarten. She would later meet us and become a very dear friend to Sheridan and me. Once again the test came. In the Pre-k program, the student is promised the same teacher through kindergarten. The district had started a Pre-k program in a new school and Sheri's teacher was to be transferred there. I went back to the Father, and then to the Principal, requesting that Sheridan be allowed to transfer as well. As always, the Father came through, and once again she was allowed to transfer. Sheridan had her two years. What am I saying? Get God in at the beginning, and He will follow through to the end.

I have not ceased to pray that God will choose all of her teachers, and now professors. Every school year I ask God to choose the best teachers for her. If a rotten egg comes in the mix, then He allows us to either have them removed or change to be of help to Sheridan. He is a faithful Father. I have learned that He wants to be involved in the small as well as the big decisions of our lives, and that is something I have taught Sheridan. Tell Him everything, ask Him about everything, and trust Him in all things. She has listened to my instructions these 20 years, and has found Him to be her best friend and Father.

Early Beginnings

As I said earlier, we started attending Faith Fellowship Ministries World Outreach Center when Sheri was about to turn 4. She went to church with me all the time. When she started Pre-K, though, I decided that I did not want to break her schedule by bringing her to church on Thursdays, so I would take her to grandmother's house on Thursdays. One Thursday night, Pastor said, "If you cannot trust God to wake your children for school, then you really don't trust Him at all." I became quite convicted as though he were talking to only me. So the next week, February of 1990, I brought Sheri to church. That was the night Sheri became filled with the Holy Spirit with the evidence of tongues. When I went to get her from children's church, the teacher asked me to sign something. I asked what had she done and they relayed what had happened, I turned to my 5 year-old and asked her if she understood what had happened to her. Her response and maturity totally blew me away. She said, "Mommy, I spoke in *Spanish* and I feel so good!"

I began to cry and she asked, "Why are you crying, mommy? I feel so good." I did not know what to do. I had not yet been filled with the Spirit. This was the turning point of Sheri's walk with the Lord. It was almost as if she had grown up overnight. I did not hear her speak in tongues for about a week. Then, one Sunday afternoon, we were both sitting in the living room and she went off into tongues, and just giggled as if she were in conversation with someone and ran to her room. Then one night at choir rehearsal as we began to pray, my five year old made this declaration, "Satan let me remind you that you will not have any place in this rehearsal," and went off into tongues. Can you imagine my amazement? I was still not speaking in tongues. It was not until December 22, 1990 before I got filled with the Holy Spirit with the evidence of tongues. God was getting ready to take both of our lives to another level in Him. Two years later, on March 5, 1992, Sheridan was water baptized.

I continued to teach her God's Word and I would pray and then ask her to pray. The maturity of her words and tone of voice were remarkable. She would take the Word of God Literally. One morning Sheridan approached me with the question. "Mommy, what does my name mean?" It took me completely by surprise. Which 5 year old child wants to know the meaning of their name? I told her I did not know, to which she responded, "I am going to pray and ask the Lord." She went to her room and came back to tell me that the Lord said her name means "Joy and Peace.' I choose to believe her, because wherever she goes she brings joy and peace.

At the age of forty-two months we were outside and I was watching a group of girls rehearse for a drill team. My little girl approached me with this question, "Mommy, do you like that?" I said, "Yes," she continued, "Is God getting any glory from it?" I said, "No," she responded, "Then what are you doing liking it?" In another instance, she had heard the song at church *He Will Not Let You Fall*. One afternoon, she was running outside and fell, and came to me crying that "He promised me that He would not let me fall and I did!" I had some explaining to do. When I would read to her from the Bible, she was taking it all in and she believed the Word. Three months into pre-k she came home with the chicken pox. She said, "Mommy, with the stripes of Jesus I am healed." She would say, "I am not going to scratch them, mommy, with the stripes of Jesus I am healed." I dressed the sores and put her to bed. The next morning they were gone. She said, "I told you, they are in me but they can't come out." In 2004, her pediatrician did a test to prove that she had the chicken pox, so I had to tell him the story. The test proved she had in fact had the chicken pox. Sheridan was also sensitive to the enemy's voice as well as to the voice of God. Two weeks after her miraculous healing, I heard her whimpering like a puppy at the kitchen table. I asked her what was wrong and she replied. "He [Satan] said that I wasn't going to get the chicken pox but I got them anyway." This was my first time teaching my 4-year-old about spiritual warfare. I asked her, "Do you have the chicken pox?" She said, "No," so I said to her, "Tell him he is a liar!" During this time the Lord would reveal to me Satan's plans to destroy her life. He would show me what means he wanted to use. Sheri would awaken many mornings to find me praying over her. I would reveal to her what the Lord had shown me and instructed her to pray over her life. If I may interject something here to parents, you must be sensitive to the voice of God for your children. Once you have committed your life and theirs to His care then you must also trust Him to reveal His plans, and anyone else's, to you.

You will notice throughout this writing I will use the phrase "the Lord told me." I do not take that phrase lightly. Allow me to make a small side trip here. I know that recently, to justify the abuse or murder of their children, mentally unstable parents have, however falsely, used this term. But for those of you who have had an encounter with the Living God, and as His sheep, have come to recognize His voice, you will fully understand without question what is meant by this statement. The God that I serve would never instruct anyone to abuse or kill his or her children. In Genesis 22, when the Lord told Abraham to offer Isaac as a sacrifice to Him. Abraham obeyed God, but before he could slay his son, in verses 11 and 12 of the same chapter, God stopped Him, and with these words we gained an understanding of the request; "And He said, 'Do not lay your hand on the lad or do anything to him; for now I know that you fear and revere God, since you have not held back from me or begrudged giving me your son, your only son.'" (Gen 22:11-12 Amp.) If you read on, you will see that God Himself provided a ram for the sacrifice. Nowhere in scripture will there be found a command of God to kill your children. That is and has always been the plan of our adversary the Devil; he has been a liar and murderer from the beginning. (John 8:44) He is the master deceiver; it started in the Garden of Eden, and is still true today. If anyone wants your children dead it is not God. Look around you today- abortion is taking the lives of our future leaders, prophets, teachers and preachers of the gospel. Who knows, we may have, through abortion, murdered the scientist who had the cure for cancer, but we will never know. All through scriptures you see Satan trying to destroy life (See Exodus 1, Matthew 2). The only instructions I received from my Father were to train her up in the way she should go. God is the giver of life! What I have learned through my encounter with Christ is just how much He desires to be involved in the intricate details of our parenting. If, like Abraham, we will obey even when we don't quite understand where He is taking us, we will always see His provision and direction. God will never shout His will, that is why we need to always have a quiet spirit before Him (1 Kings 19:11-12).

A Note On Seedlings

Throughout this book, I will endeavor to share with you only what God instructs me to. Though I will share some thoughts on discipline, this is not designed to give parenting tips. My one desire is to encourage you to raise children of the Kingdom. This is not about the strong willed or compliant child; I offer no scientific proof, just the pure time tested, unadulterated Word of God. He is my reference. So many of our children start out strong spiritually, socially and mentally but fizzle out as they get older, or go off to school. We must endeavor, as Christian parents, to try and end this spiraling down of disaster in the lives of our children. Commit to raising them God's way. Make this a top priority of your Christian walk. Commit to following through. I know it is

much easier when they are younger, but I also know something about seedlings. I love to plant things and watch them
grow. The only time I lose a plant is when I have neglected to
do something. As long as I stay dedicated to the process, the
results have always been beautiful healthy plants. Praise and
compliment your children often. Look for opportunities to tell
them how proud you are of them. Encourage their efforts in
small or big projects. Even when it does not look wonderful,
say it does. Their self worth and esteem is formed during
these times. Tell your girls how beautiful they are, and how
precious they are to you and to their heavenly Father. Fathers,
compliment your sons and your daughters often. Affirm their
outer as well as inner beauty. Be their best cheerleader. They
will never look for outside affirmation if they get it at home. I
can tell you this much about Sheridan, she knows who she is
personally and spiritually. She will compliment herself. She
does what the scripture teaches, and encourages herself in the
Lord. No one can make her feel badly about herself, but this
quality did not just happen, it was encouraged at home.

I was not taught to love or even like myself. I was criti-
cized so much that I was ashamed of who I was. But when
I really got to know my Heavenly Father, He taught me
self-worth, showed me in His word that I was valuable and
precious in His eyes. He taught me to do the opposite of my
abusive upbringing with Sheridan. So, no matter what your
past, when God gets a hold of your life and you allow Him
to become the most significant teacher in your life, He will
transform your past into a glorious future. You will not allow
your past to dictate how you relate to your children.

The seeds you plant today, the time invested, and your
willingness to go the distance no matter what, no vacillating,
will yield total victory. I can only say it has worked for me and
I desire to see it work for you, as well. One of the decisions
I made when Sheridan became a teenager was to limit my
outside commitments. I was very much involved in the choir

and other church related activities. I resigned from the choir, because that took most of my time. God used that decision to help prevent a lot of unsupervised time at home. Sheridan was able to become more involved in school activities because I was available to take her. When I started working a second job, I would sometimes get to a performance late, but, I would see her before she saw me. Looking through the audience, she would find me and a big smile would cover her face. Mommy was always there! I know you are probably saying, "What do you know? You only have one." I said the same thing to the Lord, but I guess He knew that when He told me to write. The principle remains the same whether you have one or a hundred children. The number of children God has cannot be counted, yet He wants to be involved on an individual basis. AWESOME ISN'T IT? So I guess He is not giving us an out either.

Some things are better taught than caught. Salvation is not caught. We are instructed through Scriptures how to come to saving faith, and then we are further instructed on how to live it out. Paul said "follow me as I follow Christ." (1Corinthians 11:1) I had told my daughter the same thing. That is a long-term commitment. If I wanted her to continually live for the Lord, come hell or high water, I had to do the same. Sheri prayed like a little me for a while then she learned to pray what was in her own heart. Help build godly character in your children, character that will not give up no matter what. If they see us quit when the going gets tough, then they will too. Let them see by your own conduct, that this is for the long haul. Train them up! God knew this was long term- how long has He been working on us? For me, it is now 48 years, and I still don't get it all. I have a long way to go, and I am determined to take Sheridan with me. How about you? It is never too late. If you are sincere, your Teacher will come to your aide and defense. Just let Him!

CHAPTER TWO

THE IMITATION FACTOR

I will mention from time to time that our lives are a stage and our children are the audience. You will most likely read some ideas and concepts more than once throughout this book, but know that it is more for impact, than repetition.

I know for a fact that most of what we hear children say is learned at home or due to exposure to certain television programs or associations. I made it my business to stay involved. When Sheridan started Pre-K, every child wanted a play date with her. I recall one Monday when we were off for Dr King's birthday I received a call from a father who wanted to know if Sheri could come over to play with his son. I did not know this parent, and I told him that much, and I did not know his son, the fact that Sheri did was not enough. I declined the offer. After I hung up, I phoned Sheri's teacher to enquire of this parent. She gave good reviews, but the answer was still going to stand. We had some play dates after school, each child and parent choosing their day. I would get Sheri after work. I got to know the families, visited their homes, spent time getting to know their character and what was allowed in their homes, and I let them know what we stood for. This worked very well, and Sheri was telling each of them about Jesus. This proved to be very interesting, since most of the kids she became friends with were Jews. I recall this one child in particular, which she remained very close to for about 7 years after kindergarten. Sheri would tell her of Jesus, until one day the child asked her mother for a 'Jesus Bible.' She declared that she had given her heart to Jesus and that she wanted a bible like Sheridan's. Well, the mother called me, and wanted to know what this Jesus bible was, she had told the child that she would ask her father, and he said no. The little girl did not care, she would just have to read it when she visited Sheri (they were both 5 at the time). Sheridan's Pre-k and Kindergarten teacher told of daily bible studies being held by Sheridan behind her books. She would overhear Sheridan asking the children at the table if they knew Jesus. She said, "Miss Tennant, I just left her alone." In the mornings, this is how Sheri would greet her teacher, "Good morning! Walk with the King today and be a blessing." (A line she had heard said every morning by a minister we listened to on family radio). Just recently Sheri's pre-k teacher had one of Sheri's class mates from kindergarten interning with her and she asked the student if he remembered Sheridan. He responded, "She was the one who was always talking about Jesus." What a way to remember someone!

Sheridan was not ashamed because I was not ashamed. She imitated everything I did, so I had to be careful that what she repeated or demonstrated outside the home was not a misrepresentation of who we professed to be "Christians." I recall Sheri's pre-k teacher being ill very often, I said to her, "Why not ask Sheri to pray with you sometime?" This *is* the child who prayed away her chickenpox. Sheri was quite serious about this offer. The next week after school, Sheri invited her teacher to go into the girls' bathroom with her. She asked her to kneel on the floor and raise her hands to heaven. She proceeded to ask her if she believed that Jesus could heal her, because she continued, "You have to believe

34

if you want to be healed." The teacher said yes, and Sheri continued, "Father this is my teacher. I am asking you to heal her body." All of this can be verified--the teacher received her healing, came to church the next Sunday, gave her testimony and gave her heart to Jesus Christ. They are the best of friends today. How could this be? She was just 5 years old. She had seen me laying hands on people, praying the prayer of faith as the scripture teaches, and she had done the same.

If our children are going to imitate us, why not let them imitate something that will bear fruit and bring glory to God? I have heard it said that children learn what they see and live what they learn. I do not know who said that, but it is true. I have never heard Sheri curse or swear, because she has never heard me do it, either. She knew only songs of worship and praise, because that was all I listened to. The greatest joy I have is listening outside her door during her time of fellowship with the Lord and hear her singing to Him. Early introduction to the things of God is of utmost importance. I have heard people say, "I want my children to choose their own religion." Satan is dancing in the streets to that decision. Who better to introduce your children to religion but you, the parent? That is why we have atheists today- they were left to choose. This is the age of choice, and we are allowing babies to make choices God did not intend for them to make, including whom to serve. He said Teach them in the way they should go. There is no other option.

I have often told my daughter that when I stand before the Lord, He may find other things to accuse me of, but not raising her for Him will not be one of them. I can honestly say I have not failed as a parent with no apology. I have no regrets because I followed His instructions. The glory is not mine to take or boast about, it all belongs to Him. Without Him I would not be able to write these few lines. I would not have anything to offer to this topic. He has meant everything to me, and I know that He has become everything to Sheri as well. We have become one with Him through obedience. Let this be your legacy, raise your children God's way, so that in all things He will be glorified!

What are your plans for God's children? What have you been teaching them about Him through your lifestyle? Are they learning that there is no one like Him? Would you be embarrassed if your children imitated you? Are they seeing split personalities between church and home? Do they see you reading the Word; can they make good decisions about what they watch on television or go see at the movies by watching you? Are they a good judge of character, by watching the kinds of relationships you embrace? Will they say no to sin and temptation and make godly decisions regarding peer pressure by observing you? Do your children hear you praying and worshiping God, spending time alone with Him? Can they handle a crisis by following your example? Have they learned how to dress modestly as representatives of the Kingdom? Have they learned by watching you that the tithe is holy to the Lord? The questions are endless, but so are your choices. The Bible is full of tips, if you will take the time to read it.

For young girls' parents, I remember when my daughter started choosing the clothes she liked; I would go with her to the store. If she picked out a skirt or dress, when she tried it on, I would tell her to sit down. If rode up above her knees, she was not allowed to get it. If the top was too revealing, she could not buy it. When she started going shopping alone, she was mindful of these tips. There were times when she would say, "I saw something I liked, but I would like for you to see it before I buy it." WOW! What happened here? Respect, that's what. I did not care if it was being paid for with her money. She represents my home and the Kingdom of God. Have you noticed the detail and commands God gave to Moses when He told him to build the Ark of the Covenant-in the making of the utensils, and the priest's garments, I encourage you to read about it in Exodus 25-28. God is interested in detail and excellence. We should be the same way. Remember, we are talking about imitators. Most of the clothes our children wear are bought with God's money. Yes, I said God's money. We have allowed our children to dress any way to go to God's house- this should not be allowed! We would never go to the White House in any old thing, yet that is the way some or many of us go to the King's House, so our children consequently do the same thing. The excuse is "Jesus says come, as you are"- hog wash. The High Priest had to be dressed a certain way to come before Him. Sure, you may come as you are for salvation, but after God cleans you up, the same way you get dressed for work, wearing His clothes that He provided the finances to buy, how much more should you adorn yourself to come into His presence? These are the principles I have taught my daughter. God deserves the best time, the best clothes, the best offering and the best service. All of this is taught at a very early age. I used to have parents come up to me in church and ask where I shopped for my daughter. My response was, "The same places you shop, I just believe little girls should look like little girls, and boys like boys." Children should not look like show girls or hoodlums. I believe more parents are suffering from peer pressure than children are. Sheridan never had the latest fashions because it was not necessary. We joke today that whenever something was stale or out of style that was when Sheri got it, whatever it was. Our children will learn what is important by watching us. Bottom line, parents, when you truly love someone, you will move heaven and earth to please them. God did. (John 3: 16) He gave us heaven's best in the form of His **only Son**. Why shouldn't we teach our children to give Him their best by living their best? We will never be able to effectively pass on our faith to our children if what we say does not carry over into what we do. If the script being given to an actor is not clearly written, the scene will be a mess. If the Christian life is not lived out clearly, then those whom we intend to win will be won to confusion. Let's set clear examples and give clear guidelines to one of God's most precious commodities, our children. For Jesus said it would have been better for a mill stone to be hung around the neck of the one who leads one of His little ones astray (Matthew 18:6; Mark 9:42 and Luke 17:2).

I can see why most parents would rather go it alone than seek the Lord. It is easier to take short cuts than to go about it God's way. A Christian psychologist said it correctly, "Parenting is not for cowards." It definitely is not. You will not be the most popular parent, but just hang in there; it will all pay off. Don't do it alone. Seek the face of the One who gave your children to you in the first place. If you have to ask God to change some things in your life in order to accomplish this, then by all means do it! It may call for self-denial, whatever it takes to raise your children God's way, just do it.

I never thought I would have a reason to be concerned with what came out of Sheridan's mouth because I knew what I had been teaching her, except for this little eye opener. It was the year of the *ET* mania. We have the movie at home on video. One of the characters used the (s) word. Sheridan had to be about three or so. She never repeated it, at least not to my knowledge. We had gone to my neighbor's funeral, and after the repast, we went to the supermarket. To be honest with you, I had completely forgotten about the movie. If you have seen the movie, you will recall the scene when the older brother went to the refrigerator and all that was there was yogurt. That's when he used the words "What's all this health (blank)?" Well, we were in the supermarket, and just as we got to the yogurt section out it comes, just like he said it, "What's all this health __?" I almost fainted. I exclaimed, "Where did you hear that?!" She almost fainted as she said, "From ET," I said "That's it, no more ET, you cannot repeat everything you hear, and that is not a good word." Needless to say, she is twenty, and she has no desire to see ET. We laugh about it today. Children will imitate to a fault, whether we are prepared or not. That is why it is so important for us to fill their mouths with good things, as the Psalmist says of the Lord (Psalm 103:5). Garbage in, garbage out! Don't stop when they become teenagers- the fun is just beginning. They will take your hand when you are in a crisis and need a prayer partner. One morning I found a handwritten note in my journal which read, "Don't worry mommy, the best is yet to come. This year is going to be our best year ever!" My daughter wrote that to me. I don't recall what the situation was, but I am sure it was during one of my 'Where are you Father' moments. Sheri has been a source of comfort and joy. My best imitator, she has followed me as I have followed Christ.

If I have done everything God has asked me to do, then there is no reason for me to question myself. If I had deviated in anyway from His plan, then somewhere along the way I would have created confusion. I made up in my heart and mind to do it His way; He has backed me up. If I had disobeyed, and told myself I only needed to follow on some things and not everything, I would not be writing this book today. I did not want to be the parent who said 'I praise God that even though my child strayed or tried drugs, or rebelled or had sexual relations outside of marriage he/she is back serving the Lord.' Don't get me wrong, that can be a powerful testimony. But I would prefer for my daughter to say, 'I have lived for the Lord all my life, I have never done drugs, had sex out of marriage, disrespected my mother, etc.' This is not intended to be a put down to those of you who have gone through those things, I just believe the most powerful testimony a young person can have is the one that, to the best of his/her ability, they have lived for the Lord. My Pastor often tells the story of how his mother would call him inside away from the other children, reminding him that he was chosen by God, and therefore could not be like everyone else. He has been serving the Lord for over 40 years with no testimony of backsliding. I believe that is awesome. That's the testimony I want my child to have, for it is a true demonstration of the faithfulness of God.

If you teach your children that they are special in the eyes of God, and that He has a marvelous plan for their lives, all they have to do is trust and serve Him. Show them by your examples that this is true. I believe that our faithful Father will come along side you and back up your words. He has done it for me. Our God is not a respecter of persons. He treats all of His children the same if we put our trust in His plan. I can't say it enough. Trust His plan, let Him lead, give your children to Him, let Him show you and teach you how to raise His children. You cannot fail, because He cannot fail. His Word is true because He and His Word are one. He says He magnifies His word above all His name. (Psalm 138:2) If you have done everything He has asked you regarding your children, and they did not turn out His way, I would love to hear your story. God is not a liar. What He says has to come to pass. He said He had plans for Sheri and in order for the plans to be manifested, I had to do something- commit to doing everything He said, and I didn't have the luxury of picking and choosing. There were things that I could not do, not because I didn't want to, but because my obedience was better than any sacrifice I could offer later. Disobedience caused King Saul his throne, and it would have cost me my child. See (1 Samuel 15:22)

People say to me, "You are just lucky." Luck has nothing to do with it, I was just obedient. When God showed me the spirit of rebellion, I dealt with it; when He showed me the spirit of lying, I dealt with it; when He showed me attitudes, I dealt with those; Whatever God showed me, I did not hesitate to deal with it. I sought His face and I trusted Him to lead in *all* things not some. That is why some things were just not allowed or accepted as normal. It was abnormal to allow the enemy to take over my child. She belonged to God and that is just the way it was. I gave myself no other option. It was God's way or no way. Follow after righteousness. The Bible teaches in Proverbs 10:2, 11:4-6, and 18 that righteousness will deliver us from death. Sheridan had no choice concerning her integrity and behavior-- that is, if she wanted to remain living in my house. Don't be afraid of your children! No is not a word invented by the devil, no is a good and safe word. Is it any wonder babies get that word down to a science? It is a boundary word. We live in the age of the big "WHY" There are some things Sheri did not have to ask, because based upon the principles of our home, and our relationship to Jesus, there was no need to ask, let alone ask why not. Some things are just not acceptable to Christ, and as parents He expects us to set boundaries, even as He has. Do we dare ask God Why? Take some time to go read Job chapters 38-42.

God has given us a responsibility to our children: raise them up in the fear and admonition of the Lord. There is no other option! There is no greater challenge. But He has promised not to let us go it alone. Let our children imitate Christ in us. Church attendance and Sunday school teachers should never take our place. Begin early; set the stage of love and obedience in your home by living out your love and obedience to God. I guarantee you in the name of Jesus and the witness of the Holy Spirit that you cannot fail doing what I am suggesting in this book. Begin today by asking the Lord to correct anything in your life that would prevent Him from teaching you how to raise His children. It must first begin in you as Paul said of Timothy's mother and grandmother. God Himself will restore to you all that the locust, caterpillar, palmerworm, and cankerworm have eaten. Do you know how powerful that is? Who but God can restore what has been eaten? Singles, we have the best husband, father and, friend in the whole world. Why should we settle for second best, when the Creator of the universe has willingly offered His uninterrupted, undivided love and devotion to us? Let the imitation begin! And remember, your children do not need a friend right now, what they need and are looking for are parents.

CHAPTER 3

WHEN YOUR FAITH IS TESTED, STAND!

When Sheridan was 6 years old, I noticed a small lump appearing on her upper left eye lid. At first we just ignored it but it soon became big enough to be noticed, and not just by us, but by other people. Her schoolmates would constantly ask "What is that on your eye?" Even grown-ups were asking. It got to the point where Sheridan was beginning to feel embarrassed by it.

I took her to the pediatrician and he was not sure what the growth was. It was not a sty, so he sent us to an eye surgeon who advised us that it would have to be surgically removed. I took his report to my Great Physician. We waited for the manifestation and still no change. One morning during our devotion Sheri was in her room praying, and I was in mine doing the same. I felt a righteous indignation rise up on the inside of me and I said, "Father, you did not make her with that growth, and I command it to fall off like the scales on the blind man's eyes in Jesus name!" I heard my daughter yell "Mommy!" and she came running into my room with the growth in her hand. PRAISE HIM FOR HIS FAITHFULNESS!

One Friday evening in October when Sheridan was in the 6th grade, I was making her favorite food of fried dumplings. The phone rang, so I turned the stove down and went to answer it. It was a friend of mine needing some encouragement. We were on the phone for some time and I forgot about the dumplings being fried on the stove. Sheri, unbeknownst to me, had gone to the stove to turn them. For those who have never heard of Jamaican fried dumplings, they have flour, baking powder, margarine, milk and sugar- very delicious. Well, the heat had built up in the dough because of the slow cooking, so when Sheri touched it with the metal tongs they exploded, blew the oil out of the pan totally engulfing her face, right forearm and thigh. I was on the phone and had just made the statement, "Come hell or high water, I will serve the Lord," when I heard a great explosion and the most blood curdling scream. My friend asked, "What was that?" I responded without knowing what had happened, "Satan." I hung up went to the kitchen to see my daughter curled up on the floor shaking. The kitchen was a mess. We began to pray, taking authority over the situation in Jesus name. We declared she would not be scarred. She said, "The angel placed his hands over my eyes, Mommy! He placed his hand over my eyes!" I phoned my neighbor (a police officer) to let him know what had happened and he called the ambulance. I asked to be transported to the burn center, but was told by the paramedics that they had to take her to the closest hospital-a big mistake, as you will see later. They called a plastic surgeon, and we were told that she had first, second and third degree burns. They treated the burns with silverdine and sent us home. The plastic surgeon told me to place her in the tub in the morning, wash the sores and bring her back to the hospital. He was concerned with the burn on the ear mean while, her scalp was being eaten away by a third degree burn he had missed.

When I awoke the next morning and saw my daughter I almost died. She had swollen to twice her size wherever there were burns. I called a friend of mine who is a registered nurse and I also called her pediatrician. I told them of our experiences the night before in the emergency room and what I was facing that morning. Had I put her in the tub as instructed, infection would have taken over her body. I was advised to take her to the burn center immediately. We, my friend and I rushed Sheri to the burn center where we were informed that she had third degree burns on her head and second degree burns on her face, thigh and forearm. They were amazed that she could see because of the location of the burns to her face, ("the angel covered my eyes, Mommy"). We were told that she would be in the hospital for at least six weeks, and that she would be scarred. We had already prayed the night of the accident, so I was sure that was not going to be the case. I remember Sheri praying when I had put her in bed the night of the accident that when she awoke in the morning there would no evidence of the accident. She was so disappointed, and wanted to know why God had not answered her prayer. I told her that just maybe there was someone at the hospital He wanted her to minister to. While in the emergency room at the burn center, they prepared me for the worst. She would have to be scrubbed, which would cause more swelling. We kept trusting and standing on God's promises.

The doctors were amazed at how quickly she was healing. The head surgeon said to me one morning, "I don't know how she is at home, but she is one remarkable child. She had the greatest attitude." Her face was as big as a basketball, it hurt to laugh, but she would try. If you visited, and cried at seeing her, she would comfort you. She shared her faith with all who would listen, and prayed with those who allowed her. Instead of 6 weeks, Sheridan was in the hospital for five days, she was doing so well, the doctors placed her on an outpatient schedule.

Up to that point, Sheridan had never missed a day of school since nursery school. She simply did not get sick. We had to cover the clock, because she was fretting about missing school. The only time lost was fourteen days which in itself was a miracle. She did school work from home, and then was back to school, with the bandages. She welcomed the opportunity to tell of the accident and God's favor. To be honest with you, I don't even know when the scars went away and the pigment came back to her face. First they were there and then they were gone. And I have the pictures to prove it.

The attacks on her face continued, but through it all God is faithful. She has the most beautiful smile. She lights up the room. Whatever the enemy had intended for evil, our loving Father has turned it out for good. Whenever someone says to her, "Your skin is so beautiful," Sheri will tell them the story of God's faithfulness. Just because we are walking in obedience, does not mean we will never encounter set-backs, disappointment and heartache. It is all a part of the package, we overcome by the blood of the Lamb and the Word of our testimony! PRAISE TO OUR FAITHFUL LORD!

GOING IT ALONE-It's not as bad as it sounds

As a single mother, raising my child alone turned out to be a blessing in disguise. Now don't get me wrong, I am not advocating it. You should seek the help of the father or mother of your children. God's plan is always both parents. But if God has blessed you to go it alone, count it all joy! There will be times when you will feel like killing the other parent of your child when there are things you need to be doing and there is not enough money, and you know that if the child support was coming in it would make things a lot easier, but today I can truly say I am glad he kept his money. For I can say like Abraham, that it was God who has made us rich. And I am not talking about money. That will come, because I do believe that our best days are ahead of us. Money can not purchase what we have received through obedience. GLORY!

What has blessed me the most is the continuity of the training, the values, and discipline instilled in my daughter because there was no one else to consult or the challenges of disagreement, I believe that one of the greatest setbacks of the two parent households have been the lack of agreement between parents when it comes to discipline and boundaries. The one parent thinks it should be done this way, the other that way. I will tell you something I told my mother when my daughter was 18 months old. I had corrected a behavior of Sheridan's and my mother immediately held out her arms and said "Come to grandma," Sheri came to me instead. I remarked to my mother later, "You were trying to let her think that my discipline was harsh and that she could find comfort in your arms. Sheri knows that the discipline was done in love so there was no need for her to run away from me. If you have a problem with what I did, then you say it to me out of her presence. Never interfere with my discipline or I will keep her away from you." This may sound harsh, but it was very necessary. Some grandparents can be a great hindrance to discipline. Whatever the reason, most grandparents seem to have a difficult time disciplining their grandchildren. The phrase that has now been made popular by grandparents is "We can send them home". Not in my book. Work with me. Become a team player, or lose your privilege. I allowed no one to interfere with the disciplining of my child. Rather, I gave this instruction: If you see Sheridan engaging in things that you know I would not allow do not turn a blind eye, intervene on my behalf. I have no friend who does not share the same goals for Sheridan. And I have told them that I will end the relationship in a heartbeat if I knew they did not care about her well-being. Unfortunately, there is no way to accomplish this if one parent is a Christian and the other is not. The child has to spend week-ends, summers etc. with a parent who shares different values. This can create confusion and rebellion.

As a Christian single, raising my child without outside influences was a great blessing. The power of agreement was heavenly (no pun intended). God the Father, God the Son, God the Holy Spirit were always in agreement, so I relied on their every word. For this cause, I would forfeit all child support payments. The Lord told me not to take Sheri's father to court, so I didn't. Please do not take this position automatically. I believe that they should pay to support their children. Why should a single parent go it alone while the other party bears no responsibility? This was my instruction and it has worked for me, and I am blessed to have done it His way. I know that there are others who have gone it alone, and I am sure you have your own testimonies of God's faithfulness. Isn't He wonderful as a provider? What I am saying is, if the other parent turns out to be a deadbeat, just do what Psalm 121 says, and lift up your eyes to the hills, that's where your help comes from. Our God is a refuge for us!

CHAPTER 4

HELPING YOUR CHILDREN CHOOSE GOOD RELATIONSHIPS

When Sheridan started Pre- kindergarten, I told her the importance of being and choosing friends. I told her that is was more important that one relationship be one of substance than having a multitude of shallow ones. Friendship is always built on mutual trust and respect. I told her that she should pray and ask God to help her choose the right friends and to ask the Lord to reveal their hearts and spirits. She was never to be moved by the outer appearance. This turned out to be the best advice and she did just that. I taught her the difference between an association with an acquaintance, and a friend. The scripture teaches that a friend loves at all times. Your friend will sometimes hurt your feelings, but never with malicious intentions. They will never ask you to go against your conscience, or pressure you into doing something that is morally wrong in the name of friendship. Lead by example, respect yourself, and you will be respected. Never be afraid to end a relationship if you see that it will hinder your walk with the Lord, or cause your good to be evil spoken of. The Scripture teaches that evil communications corrupt good morals (1 Corinthians 15:33) and I drummed this verse into her. 'My son /daughter, if sinners entice you consent thou not (proverbs 1:10)' God has given you a free will- use it for Him.

I am reminded of an incident that involved a friend Sheridan had during elementary school. She had invited her to church and the young woman gave her life to the Lord. They shared a great friendship all through elementary school and the first half of middle school. One morning, I came downstairs to overhear a conversation in the dining room. I overheard Sheridan telling this young woman, (and I am paraphrasing in my own words) "*I see where you have decided to walk away from the things of God to follow after the world. You have taken on an unsaved lifestyle. I have tried reasoning with you before, but it doesn't seem to be helping. So, I can no longer associate with you. The friends that I keep are reflections of my relationship with the Lord. I don't want to be known as your friend-not given the things you have begun to do.*" I know that was hard for her. This was one of her best friends. What happened? Guilt by association is just as bad as being guilty and she had chosen to separate herself. The reason Sheri's first close relationship of seven years ended, was due to the disrespect her friend and her sisters showed to their parents. Sheri had spent the weekend at their house, as had been done between our homes. This particular weekend when Sheri got home she told me she did not want to go back because the girls had no respect for their mother. I recalled the young girl begging Sheri to come over. She said no, and that she did not like the way they disrespected their mother- she never went back.

These instances from Sheri's life show that when we have instilled values in our children, they will last a lifetime. She saw that I did not have many friends. But the ones I did have, even though they were not all Christians, shared my values and respected me for what I stood for and who I am. I told her when she became a teenager that all sleep over would cease. Why? Unfortunately, this is when most parents cease supervision, and turn the reigns over to the children. They could sleep over at our house, but she would not go to theirs. I know the home I keep. There are some well meaning Christian parents who believe that teenagers do not need to be supervised. I disagree. Parents, get to know your children's friends. Do not be afraid to invite them over. One of my pet peeves was the phone calls. Schoolmates would call and right off ask for Sheri. I would respond with "If you wish to speak with my daughter, this is how it's done in my home. If I answer the phone you address me first with 'Good afternoon, Miss Tennant, this is so and so, may I speak with Sheridan please?' If you have a problem with that, you may wait to see Sheridan at school." They caught on fast. I am just as friendly with her peers as she is. They will ask about me or send a greeting home to me. I demanded respect from her friends. As a matter of fact, I told Sheridan to warn them before they called the house, if she did not want to be embarrassed.

If you choose good relationships, your children will too. Teach them how. Let them know the importance of praying for friends. Sheri once had a teacher tell her she must be friends with everyone, to whom she responded, "I may have many acquaintances, but God chooses my friends." This was elementary school. Was she correct in saying this? Sure she was. You cannot be made to be friends. Lasting relationships are built over time. Genuine friendships take time to develop. When God brings a person into your life He will also help you understand His purpose. Teach your children early on to pray to their Father for good and Godly relationships.

IS IT YOU GOD?

Trusting When We're Unsure

Sheridan began attending Rutgers Preparatory School in the fall of 1999. It was God's school of choice. We were living in Bloomfield, New Jersey and the school was in Somerset, New Jersey about 45 minutes to an hour away, depending on the traffic. This would be her first time away from home except for vacation. I knew God was sending her there when He awakened me in the summer of that year to tell me so. God did not choose Newark Academy, which was almost around the corner, (they had also given her a full scholarship), instead He showed us that He was still leading, and again tested my obedience. I cried like a baby, because I knew this meant that she would have to live away from home. But, I said "Yes, Lord, whatever you want. But where is she going to stay? It is not a boarding school." He instructed me to ask some friends of ours who lived 10 minutes away from the school. Without hesitation they said yes. I knew this was God.

We got everything ready for her to begin her freshman year. Both of us cried the day that I packed her up and took her to Somerset. Thursdays we would see each other at Church, and Friday I would get her for the weekend. This was the hardest year for both of us. I would see the sadness whenever I would take her back on Sundays, and I would cry all the way home. On Fridays she would just about jump into my arms. Despite this, I would not question the Lord. This was His doing and I would keep a stiff upper lip and walk in obedience. There were times when she would cry for me to come and get her, and it would break my heart, but I was determined to walk in obedience. God never told me to go get her, so I would comfort her and let her know that God had her there for a reason. Whatever His plans were, we would not question Him.

The school year was going well. She was not failing. But the sadness in her eyes was unbearable. I cried to the Lord. Why was my child so unhappy? Nevertheless not my will but Yours be done. I never discussed this with anyone in my church. One Thursday night I was approached by one of the elders in our church. She spoke this word to me: The Lord says to tell you go raise your child. Sheri was half way through her first year. I said alright and just pondered over what she said, never telling anyone about it. We had our home in Bloomfield. How would she get to school? The last thing on my mind was selling my house and moving. I just figured, 'good word, but God sent her there I will not be disobedient.' About 3 months had passed when the elder came to me again saying, "The Lord wants to know what's taking you so long. Go raise your child!" This time He was even more specific, "*Sell your house*, and go raise your child. Whatever you want for it you will get it. I will restore you. Just sell your house and go raise your child." I went into fasting and prayer. God had not spoken directly to me about this. Then He said to me, "If I had told you directly, you would not have believed, because I was the one who sent her there. You would have thought it was the emotional pain that was going on between you both that was driving you. I had to send someone who knew nothing of the situation." Believe me I put the elder through a barrage of questions. "Are you sure this was God? I do not want an Ishmael situation" I told her. See (Genesis 15 & 16). She went back to God, who told her not to question what He had told her to do. Well, I put God and the prophet to the test. At the end of May of that year I placed my house on the market. By the first week in June it was sold for the price I wanted. When I moved to Somerset, the Lord began to show me why He had made the request. As well meaning as the family was, who had so graciously taken her in free of charge for that whole year, there were things that God wanted done in Sheridan's life that required her mother's involvement. Only He knows what my obedience had brought about. He is all knowing, and all wise. That's why we trust Him in all things. When you can't trace His hands, trust His heart. Those were the years that the Lord allowed me to teach her about flirting, dating and building self confidence. These were the teenage years- the most important years of her development. God wanted my full participation in her life, not just on week-ends. Was the family a bad choice for her? Absolutely not! Were they capable of doing a great job? Certainly! Were they parents? Yes! Did they know Sheridan well? Yes! So what was the problem? I am her mother, she is my daughter. I know her spirit. For you see, I had prayed to know her heart. God knew exactly what that year of separation would bring. But He also knew when it would be time to bring us back together. He had not changed His plans for us. Today, I am so blessed that I listened to the words of the Elder, and went to raise my child.

CHAPTER FIVE

WHOSE CHILD IS IT ANYWAY?

Behold, children are a heritage from the Lord, the fruit of the womb, a reward. Psalms 127:3 (AMP)

When I became pregnant with my child, this scripture was not a part of my spiritual vocabulary. When I had my daughter, it was not a guide for my parenting. When she was dedicated, it was a wonderful ceremony, but this was not important to my life or plan. At the age of 30 months God reminded me that she was His, not mine. He had a plan, not me. His plan is much more noble and wiser than anything I could ever have imagined. I never could have seen or envisioned what my obedience that Saturday night would produce in both of our lives. The night I said YES to God was the best decision I could have made as a parent. As a single mom, the financial struggles were great. Her father was not supporting her and my job was not paying very well. When my daughter was 30 months old I enrolled her into day care. She had announced to me a month prior that she did not want to go to her babysitter anymore because she was bored. I decided that if she knew that she was bored, she needed nursery school. At the time my annual salary was about $16,000.00. With rent, a car payment, the school fee and other bills it was very difficult with one income. I heard that her father was saying that Sheridan was not his, so I decided to make him support "someone else's child." I retained a lawyer and he was ordered to pay $400.00 a month. This he did for about a year and a half. He asked me to work with him without a lawyer, because it was costing him quite a bit. I did, and you can finish the story. He could no longer afford the $400.00 and soon there was no money. The first time Sheri saw her father was on her 4th birthday. I guess I felt obligated to invite him since he was "paying support" He was so generous; he bought her two cassette tapes. My daughter looked at him and thought it was her uncle (her father's brother) so I said his name. She said "Daddy" then completely ignored him the rest of the time. He gave her his gift and she brought it to me without opening it. He asked me if she was going to open it. She didn't. That night after the party, I began to say within myself maybe I should get back with him for her sake. I heard the Holy Spirit respond to my thoughts. "Be not entangled again with the yoke of bondage (Galatians 5:1), I took heed. Single parents, especially single moms, heed the word of the Lord. Resist the desire to make things right for the "sake of the children." Trust Him even when the instruction seems contrary. This *was* Sheri's father, but if God saw him as bondage, then that's who he was. My request of Him was "Protect her emotions. Give her the confidence and assurances that she will need not to feel as though she is missing a part of her life. Build her self-esteem, fill her with all you are, make her all you desire her to be and pour your very being and nature into her. Cause her to be like you in all her ways. Let your mind be formed in her, give her your mannerisms, form your character in her and give her a heart like yours." He backed me up! Today, I know she is from both of us, her father and me, but she is nothing like us. God wants to raise His children, allow Him to do so! As I said earlier, her father asked if we would discontinue with the lawyers and work things out between us- big mistake, for soon the $400.00 became $60.00 and then there was no money. He had gotten behind about $5,000.00. One day while at work the Lord instructed me to write an affidavit, having him sign over his parental rights to our daughter. I was coached with every detail. I obeyed and sent it registered mail, as I was instructed. He signed and had it witnessed and returned it to me with no questions or resistance. Today I have the notarized document. God showed me his heart- he would do anything so as not to support his child, and by law if he is supporting her, then he is entitled to visitation rights. Given the life he had chosen to live, I would not have the child she is today were she divided between two different lifestyles, God is so wise!

Let me take a side trip here. We were in church one Sunday morning when my 30-month-old at the time looked into my face and said "Daddy." I shushed her to be quiet. She did it again. That night when I was getting her ready for bed she asked, "Mommy, where is Daddy?" I responded "I am Daddy," to which she responded, "No you are not, you are Mommy." So I was forced to explain to my 30-month-old what happened between her father and me. She gave the impression that she understood, so I left it alone. I called my sister in shock and asked, "When do you think Sheri will ask about her father?" My sister responded "You have time, she probably won't ask until she is 4 or so." I said "She just did." My sister was blown away. For you see, when she was calling me Daddy in church, she was trying to make a distinction between her father and myself. Just maybe if I had said yes, she would have accepted the response for the time being, and I probably would have bought some time but it was not to be. At the age of 4 God told me not to get entangled with her father, at the age of 30 months she wanted to know where he was. Her Father had plans of His own, and has coached me through each experience. The one thing I did not do was allow my own personal feelings about her father to interfere with whatever relationship she may choose to have with him in the future. I was very honest with her, but I also reminded her that because we were Christians, we had to love him unconditionally, that she was never to hate him, but pray for and love him with the same love Jesus has for us. I told her that if she ever wanted to visit him I would contact him for her. She has never asked so I just leave well enough alone. Her heavenly Father remains faithful!

When God tells you He has a plan for your children you have to trust His plan no matter what! Did I have hard times? You bet I did. It seemed to only get harder. But He remained faithful. With her father no longer an issue, I was able to devote my life to raising my daughter for the Kingdom. I literally poured the next 17 years of my life into my child, teaching and living the Word of God. I will attempt to share with you the things that God has taught me over that period of time and if you are open to some unconventional methods, you will find that it all works out and the rewards are gratifying and fulfilling as well.

Whose child is it anyway!? I answered that question at the beginning of the chapter. Our children are on loan to us. We are responsible for how they turn out. Now, I know there are some parents saying "Wait one minute, I did everything I could and my kids are a mess." Listen to what you said "I did." We do not get to decide what to do when they belong to someone else. Let's put it this way. Where do you take you car when it is broken? You would go to a mechanic. Where do you take your children when they need fixing? To the One who created them, I will never forget what Charles Swindoll said: All children are born with a God given bent and it is up to us as parents to find out what that bent is. Who knows better what He has placed in our children but the Creator? When the Lord told me to get my life together because, He had plans for my child, the next step after praying was asking Him to reveal His plans for her so I would not interfere. I asked him not to keep me in the dark about anything concerning her. I asked Him to show me his plans and also her heart and spirit. I asked him to reveal everything the enemy had planned as well, to make me sensitive to His voice in order to teach me how to instruct her in His Word. I asked him to reveal to me even her very thought pattern, so that I would be able to correct anything sown by the enemy. I asked to be shown mannerisms and attitudes. I asked to be told when to speak to her about certain things relative to her growing up years. I sought Him for direction, every step of the way. My ears were always glued to His lips for her and for me as well. I wanted to not only teach her but to live what I was teaching her. The intensity started at 30 months, but the training began much earlier.

Proverbs 22:6 says we are to, "Train up a child in the way he should go and when he is old, he will not depart from it." When I ponder those words, I am mindful of a seed or sapling that is sown into the soil. Let's think of the heart of the child as the soil. Before the child is able to communicate, he/she is busy receiving information and assimilating the information being given. They will follow us with their eyes and baby babble, endeavoring to communicate through gestures or action what they are thinking. Just as we are unable to see what is taking place beneath the soil, in the same way we are unable to see what is in the heart of the child. With the seed or sapling, we continue to water, fertilize and care for the young plant to ensure a healthy growth. Unfortunately, most parents do not realize that the steps we take in the developmental years of our children will later be manifested like a flourishing plant.

Let's take a look at the root of a plant. There are many membranous like shoots protruding from the bottom of the plant. When you place it deep into the soil, the roots not only grow down but they grow out. They are in search of a place to spread out and a place to find nourishment. Remember, we can't observe this process but we know it is taking place. Our children have the same membranous shoots as well, called the brain. Information is sought after and stored- the good as well as the bad. If the fertilizer is being poured on weeds as well as the growing plant, they will both spring up. Over time if persistency and care is not applied, the weed will choke out the very one you intended to grow in the first place.

I am reminded of a beautiful tree growing in Sheri's grandmother's backyard. The tree stands at about 30 feet. From all appearances it is a healthy tree—or it was. A while back, they had a concrete round seating built around its base. It proved quite useful in the summer for additional seating at backyard barbecues. What was not known to us was that, the tree was being stifled by what was built up around it. You might say the life was being choked out of the tree. It continued to produce leaves and appeared healthy, until one day there was a wind storm. Great big branches came ripping off and the truth of what was taking place on the inside was revealed. The tree had rotted throughout. It was not healthy at all. The tree expert informed grandma that the concrete had prevented the roots from spreading out, and had literally destroyed and choked the life from the tree. It would have to be cut down. What a waste. Ignorance had destroyed the tree's life. The healthy development of our children begins while they are but seeds. We take care to see that they have the best clothes and food, but allow behaviors and habits to go unchecked. If Godly values are not taught early on and boundaries are not put in place the result will be harmful to the child and to society. We put up gates to keep them from falling down the stairs or getting into harmful situations, yet we neglect discipline. We all benefit from the shade of a healthy tree at some point, but I have known of an unhealthy tree that has caused death or damage by breaking prematurely. To the natural, untrained eyes it appeared healthy while it had been dead or dying all along from the inside. All that was needed was a storm or wind to reveal what was taking place on the inside. If our children are not taught biblical values, they will learn the world's value system, which leads to destruction. We need to teach our children how to handle conflicts by observation. Teach them healthy confrontational techniques, all the while relying on scripture as a guide. If they witness abuse, whether verbal or physical, they will accept these behaviors as normal. Like the young plant, their lives are the roots of the young sapling seeking a place to take hold. If we neglect what is needful, they will appear to be healthy on the outside, but when the winds of life blow the results will be devastating. The bible says in Deuteronomy 6: 6-8 'AND THESE WORDS WHICH I COMMAND YOU THIS DAY SHALL BE UPON YOUR HEART; AND YOU SHALL TEACH THEM DILIGENTLY TO YOUR CHILDREN, AND SHALL TALK OF THEM WHEN YOU SIT IN YOUR HOUSE, AND WHEN YOU WALK BY THE WAY, AND WHEN YOU LIE DOWN AND WHEN YOU RISE. AND YOU SHALL BIND THEM AS A SIGN UPON YOUR HAND, AND THEY SHALL BE AS FRONTLETS BETWEEN YOUR EYES." There was never a directive to go it alone. God has given us sixty-six books and His Holy Spirit. If we prefer to lean on the arm of worldly council and our own understanding, they will direct our paths, but at our own peril. Input will always equal outcome. What is the fertilizer of your children's lives? Are you trying to be intellectually correct? Does society determine how you discipline and train your children? Are you too busy or too tired to do what is required of you? Then take heed. Where God is left out the devil will move in. A child left without discipline and boundaries is as the Bible says in Proverbs 10:1 "A disgrace to his mother." Parents, we need to remember that children are born manipulators. Yes, those cute little bundles we bring home have the sin nature implanted in them (I am not implying that babies are sinners). Everyone is innocent until proven guilty see (Romans 7: 7-20) The scripture teaches that foolishness is bound in the heart of a child (Proverbs 22:15) Have you noticed that your 3 day old baby will be fed and dry and yet scream his/her head off when you lay them down, and stops when picked up? They have begun to declare "I am here, and I am in charge." My daughter started asserting herself at two weeks. I remember I had a lot to do. I had fed, burped and changed her, held her for a little bit, and laid her down. She started screaming at the top of her lungs, and when I picked her up she stopped immediately. So I placed her back in the crib. She yelled again, but I decided to ignore her, because it was not going to be long before I had to go back to work. The babysitter she was going to have five other children in her care, and I knew Sheri was not going to be held every time she cried, so I let her cry. Now, rest assured that I made sure she was not in pain or distress. It seemed like hours, but it was actually minutes before she went to sleep. After that experience, if my daughter wanted to sleep, I could not rock or hold her; I had to put her down. A little crying won't hurt. It will probably hurt you more to hear them cry. Today she sings like a bird--Lung development is Priceless. Remember, anything will grow given the right environment, even weeds. We will reap what we sow.

A LESSON IN TRUTHFULNESS.

When Sheri was 12 months old she melted the soap in the bathroom sink by filling the sink with water and washing the soap. I found her in the bathroom with the sink full of water and the soap just about gone. I inquired of my daughter as to who had put the soap in the sink with the water. She said "I don't know." I repeated the question again and got the same response. So I said, "Do you know what your response is called?" She said no. I said, "That's lying." And I proceeded to explain to my 12-month-old that whenever she did something and denied it she was lying. I explained that there were consequences for not telling the truth and since we were the only two people living in the house, if I had not done it, then it must be her and that we would not lie to each other. I asked again and got the same response, so I spanked her legs and repeated the question. This time she responded, "Sheri did it." I followed up with, "Now, that is called telling the truth." I explained to her that whenever she had done something, that she should always own up to it even if there were consequences. Now I know what you must be thinking, "How do you expect a 12 month old to know the difference?" Let's just say age does not matter. Lying is bad no matter the age. I saw an opportunity to teach her a valuable lesson and I took it. As I write this chapter my daughter is 20 years old, and she has never to my knowledge, lied to me since. As she got older I continued to stress the importance of being trustworthy and truthful. I told her that I would never be able to defend her if she lied. But on the contrary if I can trust her word, I would always be able to come to her defense, and that her Heavenly Father would too. Parents, look for every opportunity to teach life lessons to your children. God gave me that opportunity, and against the report of most child psychologists, I taught my 12-month-old the difference between a lie and the truth. Some would say that she was too young, well praise God, my "premature" actions paid off. Take the chance. You might be pleasantly surprised at how the Lord will back you up. Whose child is it anyway?

CHAPTER 6

RAISING A GOOD CHILD VS A GODLY CHILD

1 SAMUEL 1:20 - HANNAH BECAME PREGNANT AND IN DUE TIME BORE A SON AND NAMED HIM SAMUEL (HEARD OF GOD) BECAUSE, SHE SAID, I HAVE ASKED HIM OF THE LORD. AND ELKANAH AND ALL HIS HOUSE WENT UP TO OFFER TO THE LORD THE YEARLY SACRIFICE AND PAY HIS VOW. BUT HANNAH DID NOT GO, FOR SHE SAID TO HER HUSBAND, I WILL NOT GO UNTIL THE CHILD IS WEANED, AND THEN I WILL BRING HIM, THAT HE MAY APPEAR BEFORE THE LORD AND REMAIN THERE AS LONG AS HE LIVES. V28. THEREFORE I HAVE GIVEN HIM TO THE LORD: AS LONG AS HE LIVES HE IS GIVEN TO THE LORD. AND THEY WORSHIPPED THE LORD THERE. (Amp)

This is one of the most beautiful examples of a mother who has given back to the Lord what belongs to Him

(Psalm 127:3) When we realize that our children do not belong to us, then we will trust God with the training and development of our children. Remember what I said earlier? Once the Lord told me He had plans for Sheri, I got out of the way, and began to seek His mind for Sheri. She no longer belonged to me but Him. What did He want me to do? And how did He want me to carry it out? Once I took that position, that's when the Lord began to coach me. He would reveal things in dreams, visions, and through His Word. I recall one morning while Sheri was still in Pre-K, during one of our morning devotions, I read my bible and was now getting ready to read to her from her children's bible. As I turned to the reading for the day and began to read, the Lord stopped me and said "read it to her, because this is my promise to her." It was the children's version of Proverbs 3:5-6 and it read. "If you will trust the Lord completely, and not depend on your own abilities to impress your teachers, God promises to give your teachers a special appreciation for you which will help you with your education." I can say, 20 years later that, He has kept that promise. The favor of God over her education has been awesome. Believe me when I tell you, it had nothing to do with her being at the top of her class. She has worked harder than most students to get an A B or C depending on the subject. When Sheri was in the 6th grade, a co-worker introduced us to a program called NJ SEEDS. You had to maintain A's and B's to qualify, and my income could not exceed a certain guideline. She also had to write an essay and receive recommendations from teachers. Ultimately she was accepted. The program is instrumental in getting children admitted to private high schools. They had to take the SSAT exam. Sheri's score, especially in math, was not great. Her scores were average, but every school she interviewed for wanted her. I told her to remember the promises of God, and apply wherever she wanted. We ended up turning schools down. She narrowed her choices to Newark

Academy and Rutgers Preparatory School, both offering her scholarships. I left the decision to the Lord, as to where she should go. He awakened me at 2:00 am one morning to tell me she would be attending Rutgers Prep. They wanted to know if their offer to her was acceptable to me. When God is in charge of our children's lives, He will always keep His word. He is a God of covenant. When it came time for college, I once again reminded her of His promises. Again I instructed her to apply to any college she wanted. Her SAT scores were not too strong the first two times she took them, so we took the highest scores from both to make it to 1200. I had some skeptics tell me that she would never get into the colleges we selected with those scores- I told them to hide and watch God. Even her college advisor discouraged her from applying to certain schools. I told her to apply and to let God be true and every man a liar (Romans 3:4) she applied to five schools: University of Delaware, Boston College, St Josephs University, Villanova University and Bucknell University. She was accepted to four with scholarships. We had not heard from Bucknell at this point. Her college counselor kept insisting that she apply to a safety school. I kept insisting that she had, I added "Moreover, she is going to get accepted, and it is pointless to apply to schools you do not wish to attend." We won the day. Sheri is a marvel to those who know she is not an academic goddess, but our God rules. I also allowed Him to decide where she would go. Sheri had made up her mind to attend The University of Delaware. They were offering her major and she would not have to take non-applicable courses. They could place her in her major immediately. GREAT! Everything was settled. About a month later, the Lord showed me in a dream that He wanted her in Bucknell. I told Him to tell her Himself. I did not share the dream with Sheridan. I also told Him that Bucknell was the most expensive school of all five, He simply instructed me to write to the other four schools and inform them that she would not be attending. At this point there was still no word from Bucknell. Sheri came to me two weeks after I had the dream saying, "Mommy, I want to go University of Delaware, but my heart is turning to Bucknell for some reason." I then told her of the dream. We waited a full month before hearing anything from God's choice. I got a frantic call from Sheri's high school college counselor. She informed me that Bucknell called to say that they could not award Sheri a scholarship because they were missing information- this was the first time I found out Sheri was accepted. Then, two weeks later we received both acceptance letter and scholarship information. God wanted us to walk by faith. Sheri received full tuition to Bucknell University. Like Hannah, I had given her back to the Lord, and like Samuel she had become His servant, because today she is just as committed to her walk with the Lord, as the first day she said yes to Him. Yes! She is attending one of the most liberal colleges in the USA and is living out her faith there. I will address more of this in another chapter.

LIFE LESSONS-The Training That Wins

WHEN I CALL TO REMEMBRANCE THE UNFEIGNED FAITH THAT IS IN THEE, WHICH DWELT FIRST IN THY GRANDMOTHER LOIS, AND THY MOTHER EUNICE; AND I AM PERSUADED THAT IN THEE ALSO (2 TIMOTHY 1:5) I (THE LORD) WILL INSTRUCT YOU AND TEACH YOU IN THE WAY YOU SHOULD GO; I WILL COUNSEL YOU WITH MY EYE UPON YOU. (PSALM 32:8 AMP.)

Is it possible to raise a Godly child as a single parent? YES! A thousand times yes! I shared earlier how I taught my 12-month-old the difference between lying and telling the truth. I have learned that the earlier the training, the better. I also taught her to clean up her room at the same age. Whenever she would take out all her toys, she was also responsible for putting them away. And she did. I also told her that whenever she had company, and they helped to make the mess, that if she did not have them help her clean up then she would do it alone. Believe me, they helped! You see, by the time Sheri was nine months, she had already begun to master the ability to communicate. I did not allow her age to determine her training; whether she understood or not I took the chance, and God backed me up.

Temper tantrums- not in *my* house! When Sheri started attending nursery school she began to pick up some new habits. Up to this point (30 months) she had never fallen out kicking and screaming, so I guess she saw someone do it at school, and probably saw them get their way, so she decided to try it out on me. Two days prior to the little demonstration, I bought her a hot-dog from the vendor. The next day we were on our way home and she saw the truck and asked if she could have a hotdog. I told her I couldn't get it for her. I pulled in the driveway and parked the car. I got her out of her seat and she just fell to the ground, legs flaring screaming at the top of her lungs about the hot dog. I didn't say a word. We got into the house and I told her that we would talk about that little display. I stood her in front of me and the conversation went like this:

I don't know who you saw pull that stunt today, but that will not work here. Whenever I pull the car in the driveway, whatever you have seen, or heard, except for what your teachers are teaching you, stops at the driveway. Whenever I say you cannot have something, that's the end of the conversation. Temper tantrums are unacceptable and you will be punished for that. You will never try that again. I put her across my lap and gave her a whacking on her derriere. Then I asked her to explain why she had gotten a spanking. She did. I gave her a hug, and I told her I loved her. Three days later, we saw the Hot-dog truck again. She asked if she could have a hotdog. I said, "Not today." Her response was "OK, Mommy." Picture the same scene. What if I had just allowed her to carry on, and then give in to the yelling? That would have sent the message that the behavior was acceptable. Before going to the store, this would be our conversation: Sheridan, I have made a list. These are the only things we will be getting. You will not act out, you will not ask for anything that is not on the list, and if you choose to disobey, you will be punished wherever we are. Do we understand each other? "Yes mommy" was the reply. I have never had an incident in the store, restaurant, Church or at anybody's home. The rules were established before we left. She learned at an early age that her mommy kept her word. I have never made a promise to her I did not intend to keep, and that included punishment.

Parents, I have learned from observation that our children are suffering from a lack of "following through" on our part. We say things like, "you wait until we get home" or "wait until your father comes home" or "I am not going to buy that" then we do. They have learned from an early age that we do not keep our word. I recall an incident when Sheri disobeyed me. We were at church so I told her I would address it when we got home. When we got home, she pleaded "please mommy I won't do it again," I responded "I know you won't but you are still going to be punished." I followed through. It doesn't matter if it is hours later, KEEP YOUR WORD! It matters to them that you do. They will not only respect you for it; they will also love you for it. My daughter will tell you today, whatever I say, I mean. I spoke to a parent who was returning items to the store because her 4 year old refused to wear it. She bought a jacket she could afford, the child wanted a particular kind, and the parent returned to the store to get what the child wanted. I almost fainted, and she was treating it like a joke. I said to myself, "Four!" What will he be demanding at 14? I could share many instances where I have been a bystander and observed behaviors that went unchecked. I have seen kids slap, kick, punch and verbally abuse their parents, and all I hear is "Don't do that," "Stop that, don't hit mommy." My daughter was 4 years old when she tried the hitting. We had taken my sister home from work. Sheri wanted to stop in and I said we couldn't. She lifted her hand to hit me and I promptly put the car in park, turned around and declared, "Unless you want to pull back a stump, don't you try it!" She saw something in my eyes that told her I was not playing; she almost went under the seat. She never tried that again. I am a firm believer that we reap what we allow earlier on in our children's development. All babies bite, right? I would bite right back, not to hurt her, but hard enough for her to understand that she is inflicting pain. The biting stopped. What we laugh at early on will embarrass us later. Parents, look for opportunities to correct wrong behavior. The bible says that "foolishness is bound up in the heart of a child, but the rod of correction will drive it far from him" (Proverbs 22:15) I know that in today's society, we are afraid to spank our children, but it is important to recognize that discipline and abuse are two entirely different things. I was abused growing up; I would never do that to my child. I know that some people have taken it to the extreme and have abused their children. Some have even dared to say that God told them to do it. There were times when Sheri would be spanked, spoken to, or privileges revoked. When Sheri started Pre-K, she was not allowed to watch television except on weekends. She looked forward to Fridays, because she knew she would be able to watch television. One Friday afternoon I picked her up from her grandmother's house and the hem to her uniform was ripped. Her grandmother told me that she told Sheridan to take it off so that she could mend it and Sheri said she did not want to. First I had her apologize to her grandmother, and then I gave her a choice: a spanking or no television for the weekend. I could almost see the wheels turning in her four-year-old brain. She thought about it: she was afraid of the spanking, but she also wanted to watch television. I said, "What will it be?" She quietly responded that she would give up the television. I then told her I was not on punishment so I would be watching television. We only have one television, and it is in the living room. So whenever the television was turned on, she had to go upstairs to her room. I knew that was the hardest thing for her, and the longest weekend. But she has never disobeyed her grandmother since. KEEP YOUR WORD! We have a Father who keeps His, so we should keep ours to our children as well. (Judges 2:1b) **Remember discipline without love spells ABUSE!**

Look for opportunities to teach your children though life examples. We are always trying to come from behind. We cannot close the gate after the horse has gone out. If we want to keep them in we have to close the gate now! I have learned that if we address issues before they become problems (like in the shopping incident) we will have established appropriate boundaries for our children. The Holy Spirit taught me a valuable way of approaching certain things in Sheri's development. When Sheri was six years old, we had a conversation about rebellion and why it would not work in our home. I remember it was a Friday night and we were watching television. I sat my 6-year-old in front of me and explained what rebellion was, and why it was unacceptable. I told her that my plan for her was that she would serve the Lord, and that was the plan for me as well. I told her we had rules in our home that would not be broken, and I explained that the day she allowed the enemy to plant seeds of rebellion, and she didn't think she wanted to obey any longer, that I did not care how old she was, she would not be allowed to live in our home. She began to cry and said she did no want to live with anyone else. I responded, "Remember those words, so that whenever the enemy tries to lead you into rebellion, you will know you can no longer live here." Webster describes the word rebellion in this way: An act or show of defiance toward an authority or established convention. (endnote) It's also synonymous with the words insurgence, insurrection, mutiny, revolt, and uprising. It is really intended to overthrow and disrupt any semblance of authority. No wonder God likened it to witchcraft. To me, rebellion is like a disease. The symptoms have always been there, we just choose to ignore them hoping they will somehow disappear if left alone. Most diseases or illnesses could be avoided if we would heed the warning signs. God allows us to feel pain, in order for us to recognize that something is wrong in our bodies. In the same way, He also allows us to see little habits that signal rebellion in our children. Most times we laugh at them. We call it the "cute stage." Really! How often do we ignore attitudes? Like cancerous cells in a body, if the seeds of rebellion go unchecked, they will become uncontrollable, but for the supernatural intervention of God. The Holy Spirit taught me that an ounce of prevention is better than a pound of cure: Deal with issues before they become problems!

We talked about the door slamming and the dreaded "I HATE YOU!" I told Sheridan that she would never use those words to me, and she would never slam MY door. If she disagreed with something I said, we would talk about it. The doors were mine to slam, if she wanted to slam doors she would have to get her own place. I told her she would never talk back to me in a disrespectful manner. She would never raise her voice to me in anger. She heard in my tone and saw in my face that I meant every word. Before the devil could sow his seed, I was busy sowing my own. She understood the consequences; the lines had been drawn. I told her I was not her buddy, her peers were, I was not her friend, but her mother. She did not have to love me or like the rules that were being established in our home. My God given responsibility was to be a parent, she would love me later. We would always enjoy a wonderful relationship as long as the rules were followed. Today bless God, she is 20 years and she has done none of the above. Set boundaries! It is a wonderful thing. Do it early. God will back you up. Remember, this all took place at age six.

When Sheri was ten years old, I combed her hair in ponytails. She did not want to wear it that way because she said her friends would make fun of her. So we had a talk. I asked, "Whose hair is this?" I explained that this is how peer pressure starts, with something as simple as a hairstyle. "Why does it matter what your friends think? Soon it will move from hair to something else." I explained that God had given her a mind and a will, and she is the only person that can give over her will- no one can take it. I told her that she had to be Sheri. Do you like the ponytail? I explained that the enemy would seize this one opportunity and soon she would be doing everything to please others. I told her she would be wearing her ponytails. When I got home, I received a note;

Dear Mommy, thank you for the talk, I didn't see how the enemy could take something so small and make it really ugly. I love my ponytails. What if I had missed that opportunity, and had said ok, you can change your hairstyle, I would have missed out on a very important lesson. Today she is proud of whom she is in Christ and she has not given in to anyone's pressure to conform. I have instilled in her God's values for her life.

There was another time when she wanted money for snacks. Now, I had already packed snacks in her lunch box. So I questioned her as to why she needed money. She said all her friends went to the store after school. I said, "Let's talk about that. Let's just say, a group of kids are always going into the store after school, maybe there are some who are not exactly buying, but stealing. These are your friends. The store manager had been observing this behavior for some time. The day you decide to go in with them is the day he decides to call the police. You have your money, but there is guilt by association. You do not have to be a thief to be called one, just hang around with one." I know this was far fetched, but what was she going to purchase aside from what I had already put in her lunch box? She wanted to do what everyone else was doing. She thanked me for pointing that out, as she never thought about that, and was happy with her snack. Take some time to read Proverbs 1:10 to get some more biblical insight on this point. Some of you may be thinking that I could have just given her the money. She was not going to steal. But why should I? She had a snack. God is always giving us opportunities to save our children, but we are not always paying attention. Because of what God had told me about her, I was very mindful of the "set-ups" that could come. I knew she was different because God said He had plans for her, therefore, she could not be like everyone else. God has backed me up every time.

Sheri would ask to attend different functions at school. This particular time it was a 6th grade canteen. I gave my permission to go, but told her that at 8 p.m. I would be outside to pick her up. I intentionally showed up a few minutes late. One of her teachers told me that Sheri watched the clock during the whole event. At 8 p.m. Sheri told her she had to be outside. They asked her to stay but she refused. Any other child would have come out, saw that I wasn't there, and went back inside. Sheridan stood there. Why? The rules had been established. She wanted me to trust her the next time she wanted to go someplace. I have tested her obedience on many occasions. When she would go to friend's house after school, I could set the clock by her. We have developed a relationship based on mutual trust. I can trust her word every time, and she can trust mine. But this did not simply happen, it started at 12 months. During the summer as she got older, we would see young people hanging out in the streets. I would say "Do you see that? Listen to the conversations and observe the behavior. Don't you ever let me come home and find you hanging out in the street. We have a home, invite your friends inside, but don't ever hang out on the street." She was only allowed to have company in the house when I was home. No one was allowed in her bedroom. There was to be no closing of doors, telephone usage or television watching in the bedroom. If she wanted to be on the phone, she could use the one in the living room. She understood that there should be no conversation so secret that I could not hear it, and no program she wanted to watch that I could not see. Today, we enjoy a very open relationship. We do not keep secrets. Though sometimes the thing she shares with me embarrasses me, I tell her that apart from Jesus, I am the best friend she will ever have.

CLOSING THOUGHTS

I told you earlier that Sheri did not meet her father until she was 4 years old. This is quite humorous. She went to nursery school the next day and announced to everybody that her father's name was Ricky. The people there knew that this was not true, so they told me. We had another conversation and I told her his name, and then asked if she would like to get to know him better. She responded with a question of her own. "Would *you* like to see him?" I said honestly, "No," to which she replied, "Neither do I." Yes folks, she was only 2 and a half. We tend to brag about how mature our little ones are; why not take the opportunity to make it work positively? Don't wait for them to get older to test the waters. Introduce values and habits that will be formed in their character for a lifetime. She could be a little defiant at times. If she meant to do something, and you corrected her and told her to apologize, she would rather take the spanking than say she was sorry. She would tell you right out, I am not sorry, and she would not budge. She was honest about her intentions. I respected that, but we would talk about being able to give up your right to be right. Today, even when she knows she is right, for the sake of the cause of Christ she will take the initiative to go to the person and ask to be forgiven. True humility is a gift from God. I do believe that half my battle was won when Sheri accepted Jesus Christ as her personal savior at a young age. We were able to address each situation through the lenses of the scriptures and allow the Holy Spirit to teach us.

Every opportunity was one filled with lessons to be learned and taught. I taught her to pray about everything. I encouraged her to tell her Heavenly Father all that was in her heart. We would be driving someplace and she would be sitting in the back seat having a conversation with somebody. I would inquire as to whom she was speaking to, and she would respond, "I am talking with my Father." She still does the same today at age 20. I believe we are given opportunities from birth to either mess up or do well with our children. Raising children, especially godly children, is *very* hard work. It requires spending time on our knees seeking God's face about them. Children do not come with manuals, but they come from a Father who's waiting to instruct us. We were not meant to do it on our own. I did not know of Dr. Dobson, a famous Christian family psychologist, until later in my parenting and by then I had become so dependent on the Holy Spirit that I really did not need Dr. D. When I found out about him, he would only confirm the things that I had been taught by the Holy Spirit. I just kept saying, "Did that! Amen! Praise God! Right on, Dr. Dobson." So, sorry Dr. Dobson, all my thanks goes to my Heavenly Father.

Forest Gump said, "Life is like a box of chocolates- you never know what you're gonna get." Our children come like assorted chocolates, no two are alike, but God did not make a mistake in giving us the ones we have, all we have to do is trust Him with the rearing of His children. He is faithful in all things, why wouldn't He be faithful over the most precious and valuable gift of all His creation?

CHAPTER 7

HANDLING ADOLESCENCE
GOD'S WAY

I have taken nothing for granted raising Sheri. You'll recall me telling you that my ears stayed glued to God's lips, He has coached me at every juncture. I recall one Wednesday night on our way home from choir rehearsal, when the Holy Spirit told me to speak with her about her menstrual cycle. She was 11 at the time. He told me what to say, and how to present it to her. When she started the 5th grade He told me to speak with her about sex. He instructed me on what to say what questions to ask. He is wonderful as a coach! I didn't know that sex education was about to start at 5th grade. That next week, I wrote a letter to the principal of her school asking for her to be excused from their sex education classes. I explained that we were Christians, and that the approach I would be taking to teach my child would conflict with their curriculum. He tried to discourage me by saying that they would not be able to control playground talk. I quickly responded by assuring him that because she would have been taught correctly at home she would not be taken in by playground misinformation. Parents, we have a God given right to protect our children at all costs. One afternoon, the school nurse tried to begin the discussion before excusing Sheri. She promptly raised her hand and said, "I am not supposed to be here," to which the nurse sheepishly replied, "You are right, Sheridan." I instructed the principal to be sure that my request was carried out through the 6th grade. Guess what, parents? They did!

When my daughter was getting ready for the 7th grade, we had this conversation: "I do believe I have taught you everything you need to know right now about sex and sexually transmitted diseases. I will permit you to begin attending the sex education classes under one condition, you do not ask them any questions but you will listen to what they are teaching, and bring your questions home to me." She did, and she received God's answers to life's questions. I took this same approach to Halloween. As Christians we did not celebrate Halloween, and I was not going to keep her home from school. I spoke with the Principal and explained our position. At first I was met with resistance, and was given all kinds of explanations but I held my ground. I told them she would not participate and because this was not a national holiday but a regular school day, she should be given alternative activities in school with supervision. I asked if there were teachers who did not participate and was told that the librarian was the only person. My response, she will spend that period with the Librarian. I would visit the school on that day to be sure my directive was being carried out. It was. This was elementary school. Parents we have a God given right to protect our values and our children. See you at the pole became another issue in elementary school. For those of you who are not familiar with see you at the pole. It is a student led prayer at their flag-pole. Sheri would arrive early at school to pray on the designated day. She was told by her principal that she could not engage in the activity. I got my information from The Center for Law and Justice, called the principal, gave him the facts and sent him copies. He backed off. This was elementary school. We have rights. But most of us are ignorant of those rights so we allow the government to tell us what our rights are. Educate yourselves, and act accordingly to protect your family values. Teach your children what their rights and responsibilities are. Sheri has learned to stand up and defend what she believes. She is armed with facts and information. I know that as single parents we are consumed with trying to keep our heads above water. We have more on our plates than we bargained for, and we tell ourselves that as long as our children stay out of trouble everything will be alright. Unfortunately there are other issues at stake. The wolves have been unleashed in our public school system. We need to be aware of the curriculum that is being taught to our children. Sometimes I would be the only minority parent at the P.T.A. meetings and in most cases one of the few at back to school night. Most parents will see their child's teachers once per year for parent conferences. Many times the situation is so bleak it will require much effort to right the wrongs. Single parents, make the time, I beg of you, make the time. I was determined not to fit the mold of the single, minority parent. We are often labeled as uninvolved. I was determined to frustrate their expectations. I would sometimes see the shock on their faces when I would call for a conference and show up. Every school Sheri attended they knew Miss Tennant. I stayed involved. Today, I am called upon to give talks to incoming parents, and share my experiences with parents preparing their children for college at her old high school. As single parents, we can find an excuse for just about anything, and in most cases they are justified. But when it comes to our children, there should be no room for compromise. Most will only become involved when there is a problem. Know what is going on from the fist day of school to the last. Our children's lives demand it. Their future depends on our involvement and commitment to their well being. God demands it of us, if we don't assume our responsibility as involved parents we will have to deal with the unfortunate results. In the book of 1 Samuel 2:27-36 (see also chapters 3-4). Eli the Priest had two sons, even though he had been warned of their behavior he was quite nonchalant and uninvolved. God even used a young child named Samuel to warn him to no avail. He lost both his sons, and the shock of the loss caused him his own life. I am that voice today. Do not make any more excuses! Ask the Holy Spirit to help you set priorities. Your children are counting on you, God is counting on you, this is why He has trusted you with the children you have. You don't have to go it alone. He will send the help and resources you need. Just commit to being involved. For some, like Eli, it is too late, but for others there is still time. Recently it was told on the news of a survey that was given to elementary school children regarding sexual activities. Parents were not made aware of the questionnaire. When the information became public knowledge, the parents went to court to challenge it they were told by the Judge that they were not the sole educators of their children when it came to issues of morality. No folks, this is not in some foreign country, this was in California USA. I made it my business when Sheri was attending public school, to ask for a copy of the curriculum for the school year. We need to stop things before they become an issue. The media should not be telling us what is going on in our children's school. We should take the initiative to find out. Please do not fail your children because of un-involvement. Education has nothing to do with it. Most parents believe because they do not have a college education, they are not smart enough. Common sense, I have found trumps intellect any day of the week. One man and God is the majority. Let Him lead. I bless Him for the wisdom He has given me during the critical years of my daughter's life. He kept me one step ahead of the bureaucracy, and He will do it for you.

At age thirteen I called her to sit in front of me. I asked her this question. "How old are you today?" She said "Thirteen," I responded, "The only thing that has changed is your age, everything stays the same, the rules have not changed, do we understand each other?" "Yes Mommy." Happy Birthday! I do believe parents either lose their minds or are in such a hurry for their children to grow up that they just about surrender their God-given right of parenting when their children become teenagers. Nothing has changed! You are still their parents, I told my daughter that she was not to even come to me about having a boyfriend before age eighteen, and that even then it would not be some exclusive relationship, because she would be preparing for college. She could have a friend or even friends that happened to be boys, but no exclusive emotional roller-coaster relationship. Today she enjoys the friendships of some of the most wonderful young men, who have the utmost respect and admiration for her. There are a few that she has been friends with since the third grade. They go to the movies, to dinner, the mall etc.-- no strings attached. I have met them and their parents and it is a wonderful arrangement for all involved.

Let me show you how wonderful it is to trust God with your child rearing. Do you know that even though she is 20 years old, He still tells me what to say to her about things that are going on in her life? I will just begin to speak with her about something, and tears would well up and she would say, "Mommy how did you know I needed to hear that?" Remember, I asked the Lord to show me mannerisms, attitudes etc. When she was a sophomore in high school, I went to pick her up and I noticed how she was talking to a young man. When she got in the car I said, "Let's talk about flirting." I explained the dangers of flirting, how we can unintentionally send the wrong message. I knew that she was not aware that she was flirting, but the message in her body language was. She received it with such an open heart, without an attitude or defensiveness, just "Thanks, Mom, I will be mindful of that." She was never embarrassed to tell me if she liked someone. I remember once at age 11 she asked me if it was a sin to have a crush on a boy. We had a very interesting conversation that day. I still chuckle at the memory. As she got older the Holy Spirit became even more protective of her. If I gave my permission for her to attend a function, and did not check with Him first, He would wait until she had gone to bed with my blessing, and wake me up to tell me that she could not go. My response as usual was, *you* tell her. (believe me, and you can confirm these things with Sheridan) He would. She would wake up in the morning and without fail say, "Mommy, I don't want to go. I had a dream that..." This has happened quite often. Or He would show me in a dream why she shouldn't attend a function and leave me with the task of telling her as punishment for my disobedience. But Praise God, Sheri always trusted my judgment and would not have a fit. There have been times when I have just said, "Go ask your Father, and come back and tell me what He says," I wanted her to develop the habit of seeking Him in all things, no matter what.

I remember while working a second job, I knew I had to go home early, but had no explanations why. I was getting home after 10pm every night and most times Sheridan was already asleep, so I knew that this had to be God impressing on me to go home. I called my boss and told him I would not be in that evening. I got home, and out of the blue I started this conversation with my 16-year-old:

"Just because when you are with your cousins or friends and the boys only approach and flirt with them does not mean that you are unattractive. God has placed such a hedge about you that all they will have for you is respect. They will never say 'Hey baby,' or any of the other phrases boys use to girls today, they will always be intimidated by the presence of God that surrounds you. You are beautiful, and do not let the enemy tell you any different."

Sheri began to sob, and she proceeded to tell me a story of how when she and her cousin had gone to the mall, the boys would say hi to her, but would then get into an in- depth conversation with her cousin. That afternoon she was with another young woman on the train, and a young man came over and gave his phone number to her friend, but before leaving told my daughter, "Tell your mom she is doing a great job raising you and to keep it up." This young man did not know her or me. What would make him say that to her? So I used that to bring home what I had said. "God has a hedge around you, there is a race being run for you, but only one can get the prize. God has already picked him out, so do not feel slighted, rather be proud of the fact that they respect you too much to treat you like everyone else."(Hugs, kisses, tears) Thanks Mommy how did you know that? That was just it, I *didn't* know but God did. That's why He wanted me to go home. I needed that day's pay, but I would have allowed the enemy to sow a seed that would have probably caused her to doubt her attractiveness or self-worth. We must be available to change our schedules to suit God's at any given moment.

DENYING YOURSELF FOR THE SAKE OF YOUR CHILDREN

When the Lord told me to get my act together, one of the things I asked for that night was that the Lord would take away my desire for an intimate relationship. As a matter of fact, I committed to not dating as long as I was raising my daughter. At the time of writing this book, it's been almost 19 years since I have dated or even gone on a date with anyone. I was determined to raise a Godly child with no distractions. I spent those years teaching my daughter the ways of the Lord. We had daily devotions together until she was 6 years old, then I encouraged her to develop her own quiet time with the Lord during the week. We would have devotions together on Saturday mornings. During the week I would awaken at 5:30 am to have my quiet time and then I would awaken her at 6 a.m. for her to get ready for school and have enough time to spend with her Father. She was a good reader at the time, reading on the 3rd grade level, so she would read from her picture bible or her "regular bible" as she would put it. One morning, she came to me after her devotional time and said "Mommy, you would not believe what happened during prayer! The Lord told me He wanted me to read my regular bible today instead of my picture bible and I heard Satan say 'You do not want to do that,' but I told him James 4:7 says 'Submit yourself therefore to God, resist the devil and he will flee from you,' and look what God gave to me!" It was Jeremiah 1:4-9. So, I had to explain to my 6-year-old that God had called her like Jeremiah, and that she should keep a journal of the things God says to her. It has been an amazing journey ever since. If she heard me praying for someone on the phone she would quietly walk over, take my hand and pray quietly with me. What a precious gift. We prayed together, worshipped together and walked in faith together. I remember times when I did not have money to buy her lunch meat and she would say "Mommy it is ok. I will take bread and butter or crackers and cheese," She never complained. That started at a young age as well. I couldn't get her every-thing she wanted, but her needs were met. I never made her believe that she could get whatever she wanted. She learned early on that you earned things and that you had to work for what you wanted. She learned to appreciate what she worked hard to achieve. I have often heard parents say that they want to make life better for their children. That is a wonderful plan. I too would like to make a better life for my child than the one I had. But what constitutes a "better life"? Is it just getting them more things than you had? Living in a better house or neighborhood? Better nutrition? I never saw buying my child things or living upscale as better. My idea of a better life was providing a non-abusive environment, raising her with integrity, biblical and moral values and making sure her spiritual and physical health were in tact, which would yield a better life. Clothes and shelter, no matter how modest or humble, and love and respect are all children really need. I put myself on the back burner and made sure that my child's needs for a healthy development were met. My desires and wants were tucked away until God said my work with her was complete. Dating would have to wait. My daughter was my main responsibility.

For those who may have grown up in hardships like I did, you may be wondering, "What's wrong with making sure my children have what I lacked?" I offer this response. I will sacrifice to give my daughter the best educational experiences possible, which will enable her to have the things I didn't have materially. I know families who possess the entire world's wealth and wish that they had what Sheri and I share. Do I want her to enjoy good things? Yes! But that is not the most important thing to me. We have raised a generation of children who walk around with their hands out, expecting to have life handed to them. We have majored on the minor and minored on the major in this regard. I am not against making life better for our children I just want us to have a healthy balance as well. As parents we have given so much that our children have no concept of responsibility or hard work. We have made life so easy for them that the welfare lines have gotten longer and slothfulness is now an epidemic. Our children lack motivation. They are dropping out of high school at an alarming rate. Not every child has to attend college, but they are not even willing to learn a trade. They can stay at home as long as they want, sit around and do nothing without any accountability. Something is radically wrong with this concept of 'better.' We have children

graduating colleges and coming home with this announce-
ment, "I don't know what I want to do." Where did we go
wrong parents? We gave them everything we did not have.
Now they sit at home eating our food living rent free, while
we go to work. The Bible teaches in 2 Thessalonians 3:10
that "If a man does not work, he should not eat." I told my
daughter earlier on that school was her employment. Her job
was to learn, earning the best grades she could my responsibility was to provide the environment that will help her
accomplish those goals. Her grades reflect her efforts, my
paycheck the same. Our attitudes toward our prospective
employments will determine the rewards. We have, unfortunately, treated our Heavenly Father in the same way. We
go to Him thinking we do not have to do anything, just have
faith. But the Bible teaches that "faith without works is dead.
(James 2:20) God requires something of us. Shouldn't we
require something of our children? I never tried to make up
for her father not being there by buying things that we could
not afford. *Parents, growing up without a mother or father is
not a disease or the end of the world.* We make the mistake
of replacing values with things. Sheridan appreciated my
time with her more than anything I could have purchased.
If I told her I couldn't afford to buy a new dress for her at
Christmas, she would say, "That's all right, Mommy, my
clothes still fit." I would make the sacrifice and surprise her
at times and she would be so appreciative. Today, if you give
her a pencil, she behaves as though you have given her a
diamond ring. She would ask for extra offering money for
church when she was in Sunday school because there were
some children who would come without. She would give the
dime and give them the quarters or dollar. She did not know
which was more valuable, just that everyone had something
to give. She gave away one of her bibles because there was
a child who came to church without a bible. She was just
six and seven respectively during these events. She learned

to give by watching me. We are actors on the stage of life parents, and our children are the audiences. They will imitate the good as well as the embarrassing.

At the time of this writing I had my 48th birthday. I am still single and have not dated. The results of my sacrificial obedience has paid great dividends. Sheri is everything I had dreamed and more. We will never fail keeping our promises to God, and He will never leave us alone. Our children will rise up and call us blessed. You have heard the saying he who has the most toys win, this is not true in parenting. Seek His heart in all things.

CHAPTER 8

LESSONS ON GROWING WITH YOUR CHILDREN

Children will learn humility and respect from us. I have had to apologize to my daughter on many occasions. When I may have said something that I did not realize hurt Sheridan deeply, the Holy Spirit will make me aware of her sadness, and noticed that she would become very quiet. I would approach her and ask her if I said something that upset her. I would hear her out, and then apologize to her. That act, I believe, has cemented our relationship. She knows that I will admit when I am wrong and ask her forgiveness. If I have to correct a behavior, and she became upset, I would give her the space to deal with it, but I would never permit her to go to bed upset with me. I would go to her, and ask if she is alright. She may say she was fine. I would continue, "You are upset with me, and I can understand that, but I will not allow the enemy to cause you to be bitter, so come give me a hug." She has never, to my knowledge, gone to bed angry with me. Take some time to read Ephesians 4:26.

I have often heard new parents say, "Oh, she's got me by my heart strings, and she knows it," and "How can we say no to that face?" And I'd say, "You're gonna get it, you're gonna get it!" Psychologists say we have two kinds of children, the strong willed and the compliant. Our Creator only sees one personality type of all His children: We are all born in sin and shaped in iniquity! So how do we move past the cute to the truth? We allow the Holy Spirit to guide us past our flesh and fantasy, to deal with reality. The little cuties will grow up, whether we like it or not, and if we do not follow the will of God for our children, they will be a cute mess! Judges 13: I will pick it up in verse 7 -please read the entire chapter when you have a chance, it is most fascinating-

> *But He said to me, behold, you shall become pregnant and bear a son. And now drink no wine or strong drink and eat nothing unclean, for the child shall be a Nazarite to God from birth to the day of his death. Then Menoah entreated the Lord and said, "O Lord, let the man of God whom you sent come again to us and teach us what we shall do with the child that shall be born. And God listened to the voice of Manoah, and the angel of the God came again to the woman as she sat in the field, but Manoah, her husband, was not with her."*

I could write the whole chapter, it is absolutely wonderful. Do you understand what has transpired? The woman told her husband of the encounter, he prayed to be let in on the instructions, God heard, came again to the woman, she ran to get her husband, God reiterated the instructions given to his wife and the power of agreement took over. One of the greatest hindrances to good child rearing is disagreement between parents. We see that the child belongs to God before conception and He will give specific instructions for His will to be carried out for our children. We see the importance of both parents being involved in the child rearing. And finally we see the willingness of God to participate in our unity so that the child will not have any opportunity to play one parent against the other. Both Manoah and his wife received the same instructions. Parents, there is no wait "until daddy comes home." In the aforementioned scripture, we see that God first gave the instructions to the mother. Mom, your role is of utmost importance. You are the nurturer, why do you think God allowed Pharaoh's daughter to return Moses to his mother to be reared up? Why do you think Hannah refused to go to the temple until Samuel was weaned? The sensitive first years are in the hands of the mother. The father, if willing (like Manoah) will be introduced into the plan of God as a participant. His role is to support the discipline of the mother, and to give clarity to what has been taught. Whenever a child gets the idea that he can manipulate one parent over the other, the battle is lost. The wisdom of Manoah will serve father's well. He was not upset that God had gone to his wife first, rather he wanted to know that he fully understood God's plan, and that his wife had his support to carry out whatever God had commanded for their child. He prayed to be let in on the plan of God. What an awesome act of humility and surrender to the plan of God for the child. That was what I spoke of earlier, the importance of hearing God's voice for your child, following His every command. He is the Creator and the owner. Let Him instruct you. What a privilege to have God care so much that He would take the time to instruct us as to how to raise His children. GLORY TO OUR AWESOME FATHER!

So many mistakes in child rearing could be avoided if parents took the time to follow the instructions laid out in Scripture. The Bible is filled with the guidelines necessary for raising our children God's way. There is no room for compromise, we have to mean what we say and say what we mean, even when all of society says we are crazy. I recall being told by a well meaning parent that I needed to take my head out of the sand when I said I would not allow my teenage daughter to come home whenever she pleased. I told her that her head was so deeply buried her child was practically raising herself. I cannot imagine any Christian parent wanting to raise their children independent of God's help. We do not need intuition; we need the Holy Spirit. We do not need more books, though there are some good ones, we need the "Good Book." We do not need a village, if the village misrepresents the values of Scripture; we need God's instruction manual. I'm reminded of a song, "Give me that old time religion." If it was good for Paul and Silas, then it is good enough for me. We will buy every child-rearing book that comes out, while ignoring the time tested Word of God. I hope this book sells, but more over I hope that it will only lead you to The Bible, and to total reliance upon the Father of all Fathers to help raise your children. No, babies do not come with a manual, but after reading Judges 13 and 1 Samuel chapter 1, I am convinced that all the instructions we need comes when we get on our faces before God and ask for His help. If he showed up for Manoah, He will show up for you too. Just ask me how I know.

Baby dedication is important, but most of us miss its significance by getting caught up in the moment of cute dresses and handsome suits. What we are actually doing is giving the child back to the Lord, the way Hannah did. As soon as the child is able to understand, we should begin to instruct them in the ways of the Lord. My prayer for my God-child and your children is that they will learn about the Lord not at church, but at home. They will not learn to pray at church, but by observing you. They will learn to worship, not at church but by seeing you worship. They will learn how to tithe, not by hearing their pastor talk about the importance of giving, but by watching their parents put God first in their finances. They will learn to love His house and His people by observing your faithfulness to church attendance and your interaction with people. It is up to *us*!

It pains me to see parents rely on the church to instruct their children in the ways of God. Let the church serve only as a confirmation to what you have already taught them at home. When Manoah wanted to know what to do, the Bible does not say he went to the Priest, but that he entreated the Lord. It was important for him to know and understand what to do with the child. The result was God showing up in response to his request. Are you willing to entreat the Lord on behalf of your children? Or do you think that you can do it alone? The best way is His. Allow Him to do his job. He did not mess up raising Jesus, and what an example and legacy He has left for us. Jesus did nothing without consulting with Daddy, why should we?

CHAPTER 9

WHEN GOD GIVES US OPPORTUNITIES, TAKE THEM

Don't Back Down

I said in an earlier chapter that we are always given opportunities to teach our children life lessons. They can come in small insignificant ways or in big ways. I told you of the ponytails, the snack money, flirting, and self doubt. When God has given you the spirit to discern certain behaviors or attitudes in your children, don't put off praying about it, pray immediately. Stop to ask, "What is it, Father?" and wait for His responses. He will always let you know why He is allowing you to be aware at that particular time. It is said that on the day of 9/11 there were people, who for whatever the reason, were either late or decided not to go to work that day and thus their lives were spared. I believe in divine appointments. God will set us up, and most times He is testing our obedience. The scripture teaches in John 10:27 (Amp.) "The sheep that are my own hear and are listening to my voice;

and I know them and they follow me." When you have dedicated your children to the Lord, the one proof of that is your willingness to always listen for His voice, committing to do whatever He says, even when it is not popular with those around you. Even well meaning Christians will disagree with you. They will say, "This is the 21st century, he/she is a teenager. Rebellion is natural." Incidentally, rebellion does not begin in the teenage years, it started long before then. My response to those statements is, show that to me in the Bible. They will have to make their own mistakes, true, but to what extent? I've heard, "it's ok for them to backslide, remember the prodigal son, he came back," and this is true, but how much hog food did he have to eat and how much filth did he have to wallow in before he came to his senses? Why would you want that for your children?

Jesus said, "Suffer the little children to come unto me, and forbid them not for such is the kingdom of heaven." (Matt. 19:14, Mark 10:14, Luke 18:16) Let me paraphrase. Bring your children to me early; don't set up obstacles in their path, for heaven belongs to them when they come as children. Backsliding was not an option in my house, nor was the opportunity to rebel as a teenager, and making willful stupid mistakes. I left no room for any of the above. In Luke 2:48-52 it says that,

"And when they [Joseph and Mary] saw him, they were amazed. And his mother said to him, 'Child, why have you treated us like this? Here your father and I have been anxiously looking for you.' And He said to them, 'How is it that you had to look for me? Did you not see and know that it is necessary as a duty for me to be in my Father's house and occupied about my Father's business? But they did not comprehend what he was saying to them. And he went down with them and came to Nazareth and was habitually obedient to them and his mother kept and closely and persistently guarded all these things in her heart. And Jesus increased in wisdom (broad and full understanding) and in stature and years, and in favor with God and man."

"How is it that you had to look for me?" What a question. "You have taught me what is needful, why would you expect me to be any place else?" Because they did not get it, Jesus submitted to their authority until they did. His obedience produced wisdom, and favor both with God and man. Now that Sheridan is away at school, I don't sit up at night worrying about where she is, and what she is doing, I have trained her in the way she should go, she has not departed from it, and I expect her to be about her Father's business. I said there was no room for what was okay by the world's standards. I stuck with it. I informed my daughter at an early age that I was raising her for the Kingdom of God not Satan. I had made up in my mind to follow Jesus, and neither she nor the devil was going to be an obstacle. I reminded her of the commitment she had made to Jesus and that even though I had been a backslider at one point in my life that was not a choice I suggested she make for herself. I explained backsliding, and how it can create a barrier between her and her Father, that the sweet fellowship she now enjoys would be broken, but most of all it would break His heart. The scripture says we crucify Christ again. Hebrews 6:6 says " *If they deviate from the faith and turn away from their allegiance it is impossible to bring them back to the repentance, for because, while as long as they nail upon the cross the son of God afresh as far as they are concerned and are holding him up to contempt and shame and public disgrace.*" OUCH! If we are brutally honest with our children about what separation from God does to our lives, they will consider their decisions. If Jesus is real to us, and they saw that growing up, then when they make a decision for Christ they will not backslide. There is so much compromise at home that children are being sent the wrong message about what a committed relationship to Jesus really means. I never gave my daughter an out. If God said it was wrong then it was wrong for me too. I taught her, what rebellion meant, and how God dealt with rebellion. He likened it to the spirit of witchcraft. 1 Samuel 15:23. Don't be afraid to teach the scriptures to your children. Let them know that if they reject God, He will also reject them. It is harsh but true. I have told my daughter that not everyone has the story of the prodigal son, there are some that have backslidden never to make it back, and therefore, it was not an option. I did not invest my life in raising her up to see her walk away from the truth of God's word. When God told me He had a plan for her life, I said like Manoah, "Tell me what is required and I will do it." I did not look back, I have not deviated, and neither will she. The scripture teaches that obedience comes with a promise. I have taught her that principle as well. I have told her that I will never ask her to lie or cheat therefore every request will be based on mutual trust and integrity. She has learned that my word can be trusted, that if she will honor me as her mom, and walk in obedience she will be blessed and obtain favor from God and man. Guess what? She walks in God's favor continuously.

I have always been open and honest with my daughter; there are times when the Lord will have me share details of things that I have done in my past. Then He will use the opportunity for me to instruct her in not making the same mistakes, especially things that can easily be avoided. I have often told her that I had made enough mistakes for both of us. I can hear the rumblings now. Nobody is perfect. I emphatically agree, I have more flaws than anyone, but never be afraid to share what the Lord tells you with your children, He does have His reasons Most parents are so ashamed of their past, that even when it will help someone (their children) they will not obey the Lord and open up. They already know that we are not perfect so what is the big deal! There are times that the Lord knows that if He had given me a warning that He wanted me to share a particular thing, I probably wouldn't, so He would set me up during our devotional times together. Emotions are high and we are just singing love songs to Jesus and it all comes out. (I said no secrets) He said no secrets. It has made us closer and stronger in our relationship with each other and with our Father.

Use every opportunity He gives you. He will always come through for you. Before my daughter left for college, I was having my quiet time with the Lord as I always did in the morning. As I was preparing to read Micah 6, the Lord instructed me to share verse 8 with Sheridan. It reads "He has showed you, o man, what is good. And what does the Lord require of you but to do justly, and to love kindness and mercy, and to humble yourself and walk humbly with your God?" It was very clear from the scripture that everything that I needed to do had been done to prepare her to go away to college. After she read the scripture I told her this:

> *"I have obeyed in all things what the Lord instructed me to do in order that you can live for Him. The plan of God for your life can only be hindered by your willful disobedience. There is no more teaching, just admonition. If I have failed in any way, may the Lord reveal it, but it is clear today that the Lord is saying I have done what He asked. Now, it is up to you, I have heard of and seen 'Christian kids leave for college and return cold and indifferent to the things of God.' Before you make such a decision, turn down the scholarship to Bucknell and take a job at K-Mart. You will not become a statistic. You will live for the Lord! God has chosen Bucknell for a purpose."*

When He told me of His choice, I willingly submitted to His plan by saying that if it was even for one soul on that liberal campus, it would be worth it. I only had one request of the Lord—that he would hold the snow when I had to get her from school. He has been most obliging. Today she lives for the Lord on campus. Backsliding?! Not an option. One of the first things we did when we arrived for orientation- at her suggestion I might add- was to check out the religious life on campus. We spoke with the people in charge of religious life on campus, and I asked to be e-mailed copies of their weekly sermons. I told them I wanted to be sure we were on the same page. What I was being sent was biblical, what I was missing was the presentation. One Sunday afternoon I received a phone call from Sheri, informing me that she would rather stay in her room and listen to the tapes I sent her from our home church than go to chapel. I asked her why and she said, "Mommy, the Word, is being compromised" then she went into details. I suggested that she check with other older students who went to church off campus to see what other options she had. Well Glory to God, she now attends a Church like ours called Revival Tabernacle, fifteen minutes away from campus. I have gone several times on my visits to Sheri at school. What a blessed place to serve the Lord. The pastor and his wife have embraced the students who attend. They are involved with their campus ministry and have been a source of spiritual, emotional and financial blessing to the students. God has left no stone unturned. Faithful is what He always has and will be to us when we put Him first.

I believe that Christians, as well as the unsaved, set their children up for certain acts of rebellion, by buying into the idea that it is normal. How does God respond to the world's concept of what seems normal? Absolute folly! (See 1 Corinthians 1:18-21) The Bible does say however, that "foolishness is bound in the heart of a child, but the rod of correction will drive it far from him." Proverbs 22:15. I know that most parents fear Division of Youth and Family Services more than they fear God. Whose child is it anyway? I had a saying: I had never heard them knocking on my door when she needed food, clothes or shelter. The day they take on that responsibility, they can tell me how to raise my child. Don't get me wrong, they are a necessary evil. Some people do abuse their children, but more abuse takes place under their watch, and research will support my claim. How many children have you personally killed by discipline? How many children have died in foster care? I would tell my daughter I am the Division of Youth and Family Services, if they can do better, they are welcome. Whenever I had to discipline her, I did. At 20 years old, she has never been in trouble with the law, I haven't been called in to school because of disciplinary problems, but I have been called in because she was witnessing in school Pre-K through 6th grade. As she got older she did not need my defense; she handled her accusers on her own. If I am going to be called in for anything, let it be that. I recall one evening going to get her from school. She was in kindergarten, the teacher said she was a little restless that day and suggested that maybe she was having a bad day. I responded 5 year olds do not have bad days. I have bad days. The one thing I have noticed since moving to the United States 26 years ago is that we have a name and an excuse for everything. Personally, I think most times it is a cop-out. We won't have to deal with it if we can explain it away. Give them some medication, they are from a broken home, they are from a single parent home, their parents are divorced. Excuses, excuses! Don't get me wrong, there are some legitimate cases, but most are just excuses. Deal with things early on in life and they will not become monsters later. I said before, I gave my daughter no outs.

She was never allowed to raise her voice to me, storm away and slam doors, tell me how much she hated me, or disrespect me in any way. It was just not allowed. These were things we dealt with very early in her development. Before they ever presented themselves as an issue, we dealt with them. After each talk, I would say, "Let me tell you what the consequences are, just in case you allow the enemy to sow the seed, so you will know way in advance why it will not work." I never backed down; she always knew where I stood on all issues, because we communicated. Did we have disagreements? Plenty. But we handled them in a respectful way. If she needed to express herself, she did not yell, we spoke respectfully to each other. If I raised my voice in anger, the Holy Spirit would let me go on, and when I was done, He would let me humble myself and apologize. I will give you an example of what I am speaking of. We were on vacation in Puerto Rico. The oldest child of the family we were visiting wanted Sheri to go someplace with her. She had just received her license and I was not comfortable with the idea, neither was the girl's mom. I told Sheri she could not go. As teenagers are known to do, they kept pleading their cause. Sheri knows that once I have said no to something that makes me uncomfortable I do not change my mind. They kept it up until I lost my cool and did something I said we would not do. "I yelled at her." She was embarrassed and humiliated. We went into the City that night and she was quiet the whole time. The Holy Spirit instructed me to speak with her about what had transpired earlier, to apologize for my outburst and ask for her forgiveness. Respect was mutual. It was not due me, I earned it by practicing what I preached. Do not give in to the lie that if you establish boundaries for your children, they will not love you. They will later. It is not about their love for you; rather, it is all about your love for them. Follow the Leader. God loved us so much He made sure we had a future through the sacrifice of His Son. Jesus was misunderstood and hated, but He still did what was necessary to bring us eternal life. We did not appreciate it at first, or understand His reason for doing what He did, but when we "grew up" we embraced His sacrifice with joy and gratitude. Our children will too. Remember, it is not friends that they need, but parents. Stick to your role it will eventually pay off.

UNCOMFORTABLE SUBJECTS

Every opportunity is God given. It's when we take advantage of them that we can build or destroy relationships with our children. I don't judge my daughter, nor do I take her for granted. I sometimes talk with her as though she were doing what we talked about at the time, not in an accusatory tone, but more along the lines of 'you are capable of doing it.' I have taught her never to be afraid of sharing everything and anything with me. I said earlier that sometimes she embarrasses me, but hey, I got what I asked for. I would rather be embarrassed than have her go to someone who does not have her best interest at heart. If you are truly trusting God with the development of your children, everything is fair game. He, the Holy Spirit will guide you into all truth. (John 16:13). Whatever you lack in your own strength, He will come to offer help. It's amazing how much He knows about current stuff. He is not afraid to talk about SEX. After all, He created the act; who better to ask for advice and information? I am not ashamed to talk to my daughter about sex; as a matter of fact when she was quite young, He told me to talk to her about the subject. Do not be so ashamed or embarrassed that you allow the devil's crowd to educate your child on one of God's most wonderful gifts to married couples. Open the Bible and teach it to them God's way.

You know I said earlier that I had Sheridan out of marriage. To be quite honest, I did not enjoy sex that much, because one night the Lord showed up at the foot of my bed demanding to know what was I doing to His temple? That ruined it for me. Believe it or not, I was a backslider at the time. When God says He is married to the backslider He wasn't kidding. I had to tell her all of this, and the importance of doing it God's way. I laid out the reasons why. First of all there is no shame attached to sex according to God's guidelines. You are not afraid of getting pregnant, and you will be more confident, especially if you have saved yourself for your husband. The purity of the act invites the blessing of God. Hebrews 13:4 - reads (amp) "Let marriage be held in honor (esteemed worthy, precious, of great price and especially dear) in all things. And thus let the marriage bed be undefiled (kept un-dishonored); for God will judge and punish the unchaste (all guilty of sexual vice) and adulterous." When you teach this to your children, if they have a heart after God, even if you have messed up in the past, they will not be inclined to repeat your mistakes. Parents, just be real with your kids. They are like little bloodhounds, they will sniff out the truth and if you have not been honest, they will never trust you. Answer age appropriate questions as candidly and honestly as you possibly can. I would always say to my daughter, after having an important discussion, "Repeat to me what I have said and explain to me in your own words exactly what you understand of our conversation." As she got older, there was no need for that approach, but prior to the teen years that approach worked well. I did not want to give her more than she requested, but at the same time I wanted to be sure that we were on the same page. God was and is faithful. What the Lord told Joshua is still relevant today. "This book of the law shall not depart out of your mouth" (Joshua 1:8.) and the Israelites in Deuteronomy 6:6-9. If we bind the Word of God on the tablets of the hearts of our children, guess what will happen? They will tell the devil: "Because I have submitted myself to God, I can resist you and command you to flee." (James 4:7) They will not stray, they will obtain favor from God, their days will be long, and they will rise up and call you blessed.

Risk it all on God. Do what He says even though it may not be popular. As long as He approves, who cares what the world says? If God says it, that settles it! Your teenager does not have to lose his/her mind. They do not have to rebel, backslide, do drugs, have pre-marital sex, or disrespect your home. At 20 years of age, I am still waiting for my daughter's terrible two's, the temper tantrums, teenage rebellion, and the disrespect I was told to anticipate. But, it never happened because it was not an option! Why have we become so afraid to discipline our kids? When one of God's kids rebelled, Jesus said of him "I saw Satan fall from heaven like lightening." (Luke 10:18) I guess that was some kick in the pants! Parents, we will reap the fruits of whatever was allowed. We all have choices to make; I can only share what God has taught me. It has worked. I am not an isolated case, and I am not special, nor do I possess special gifts. I have just learned how to let God be God and allow Him to do His thing. All you have to do is recognize that you are not the giver of life, He is. You only know what He has given you the ability to comprehend. If you trusted Him for salvation, why can't you trust Him with your children? (Proverbs 3:5-6)

CHAPTER 10

PASSING THE FAITH BATON:
Reaping your Harvest

By now you have a clear understanding of where I am going with this book. I am sure to some it must seem like Sheridan is only serving God because of me or the fear of losing her life. Well that is not the case. One of the most important decisions anyone can make is to ask Jesus into their hearts, receive Him as Lord, master and owner of their complete lives. I shared that Sheridan accepted the Lord at the age of 5. That was early, and most children will either continue on in their faith or have no clue later as to what took place. The key to keeping this from happening is to become a mentor to that young child by teaching them the Word, and demonstrating openly by your own conduct what it means to live a Godly life consistently. Will you hit some rough spots along the way? Surely. But the way we handle these situations will be very important in the early development of your child's personal relationship with Jesus.

Sheri has seen me go through some rough times. She has heard me crying out to God in difficult times, she has even heard me complaining to Him. She has witnessed times of real highs and disappointing lows. But through it all she has a seen my consistency to follow Jesus no matter what. I never presented a false sense of what the Christian life is all about. It *is* life! It is *real* life! Jesus Himself said it would not be without trouble. There were times when I had no song, and I had to ask God for one. I did not feel saved sometimes; I knew I was, I just did not feel like it. Guess who would come alongside me to bring words of comfort? You guessed it, Sheridan. I would find scripture in my wallet, or under my pillow-the seeds I had sown were coming back. I explained to her as a little girl that during Pre-K to 6th grade she would find it very easy to share her faith. She would face little opposition. But as soon as she entered middle school, she would discover that those children now had an opinion, and that it would not be as simple. I explained that at times she would not want to share her faith just to avoid confrontation. This was the real test. I would spend time with her in the word, pray with her and encourage her not to be ashamed of whom she was in Christ, because He would be ashamed of her. I encouraged her to do less talking and more living. I told her to let her life speak for her, then the questions would come, and she would have an open door. I told her God would cause her to stand out like a sore thumb, He would show her to be different. I told her not to blend in, but to stand out and she did.

On a side note, one of the things I most admire in my daughter is her willingness to listen. She has a teachable spirit. I tell her often how thankful I am for that quality, and that I do not take for granted the things that she does even at her age. Parents, this is very important. When, at 20, she will still ask permission to go out with her friends, I let her know that I appreciate that gesture of respect. It is very important to do that with your children, especially teenagers. While most kids do what they want because they are in college and supposedly grown, my daughter still respects the rules of our home, and I thank her for that often.

Now back to the topic at hand. Sheri came to me not long after we had our conversation about the hardships of sharing faith as she and her peers got older and said, "Mommy, remember when you said as I got older it would become more difficult for me to share my faith? You were so right." So we talked about that for a while. What if I had not discussed that challenge with her earlier on? It could have proven to be devastating. The difference was she was prepared. God will do that. He does not walk away when they become teenagers and say "You are on your own." This is when we need help the most. In most cases they have become who we were and it is downright scary! Just remember, help is just a prayer away! I recall someone saying to me, "Wait until she becomes a teenager." As usual I responded, "I can't wait to see the woman of God she will become as a teenager. If God has done this much already, I can hardly wait to see what else He has in store for her. When Sheridan started high school, I said to her, "You have been such a good child up to this point, do not go to high school and lose your mind." This was her response, "Why would I want to do that? This is the next step to determining my future career path." I rest my case. She had received a scholarship to Rutgers Preparatory School. This was definitely not the environment for the faint hearted. If you did not possess much by way of the world's wealth, it was in full demonstration on this campus. This never became an issue, she was raised with Godly values, and possessed great strength of character. She was never a follower, always a leader. I had told her often, "You may lead, because you know where you are headed, but never follow. Lead them to Christ by your conduct." Ask anyone from her schools what they remember most or admired about Sheridan, from Pre-K to High school and they will all tell you the same thing: Her commitment to her faith, and the high moral standards to which she held herself. This blesses me, and all Glory goes to God because He led and I followed.

When Sheri was a sophomore in high school I asked her one Sunday as we were driving home from church "Why do you serve the Lord?" Believe me, I waited for her response with fear and trembling. If she had said "because you make me," or "I am afraid of what you will say or do," I would have failed miserably at passing along my faith. Instead my beautiful baby said, "In the beginning, it was because of you, but as I got to know the Lord more intimately, I knew it had to be my decision to follow Him, you have taught me how to trust and serve Him by being a living example, but now I know and love Him for myself and I desire to serve Him." WHEW! If she had said anything else, I would have had to ask her for forgiveness for failing her and God and I would have had to start all over trying to find out where I had missed God. Praise God all is well.

You can lead a horse to water but you cannot make him drink. The same is true of passing our faith on to our children. You cannot teach what you refuse to live. God will not back up hypocrisy. But He will always honor faith. Sheridan was not exposed to one way of living at home and another at church. I once had a co-worker of mine tell me that she purposely came to my home at different times unannounced just to see if she would find me being anything but a Christian. Well guess what? She didn't. I honestly do not know exactly what she was looking for, but whatever it was, she did not find it. Do I blow it from time to time? YES! But there is always a place to begin again. It is called confession. God is not surprised, disappointed yes, but never surprised. The best lesson you can teach your children when it comes to your faith is to live it. If Jesus is really Lord, live it. If He is your all in all, show it. Singles, if He is the lover of your soul, live like it. If He is your provider and your only source, show it by example; don't try to find a man to be to you what only He can be. My daughter has never seen me with a man since the day I got on my knees and repented before God. No one has played with our emotions. We belong to the Most High God; He will sustain and provide for us. Even when we are at the bottom of the barrel and the cupboard is bare and the bankbook is empty, He remains faithful. He will provide. Don't just teach it, live it, and they will too.

CHAPTER 11

LETTING GO GOD'S WAY

GIRL TALK

When your child confides in you, do not reveal it to anyone. If it is something that they do not mind sharing then that's alright. There are things that Sheri and I share that are strictly confidential. I mentioned before that we talk about everything. The Lord will still share things with me, and we will talk about it. I have asked the Lord to help me to know when it is time to back off and begin treating her like a young woman; to let me know when to give my advice or opinion etc. As parents we always have an opinion, but I needed to learn when not to have an unsolicited opinion. Now instead of asking for guidance to raise her, I was asking for guidance in learning how to let go. I was still being asked for permission to do things even while she was in college. At 20 years of age I knew I had to start allowing her to make some decisions on her own. So I prayed and asked for help. I remember her calling to say that she would be going to visit a friend from high school in Philadelphia. My question was, "How are you getting there?" I was told that one of the girls had a car and they would be driving. Well my parental antenna went way up. "You do not own a car, what if there was an accident, you have caused someone else's child to get hurt," the answer was no. She did not say anything then. Later, she called back, and said the following:

"Mommy, I want you to hear me out without saying anything until I am finished. I didn't have to tell you of my plans. Most of the kids here don't tell their parents anything. You are treating me like a child, and I have not done anything to cause you not to trust me. I did not like the tone you took. I know that you had a rough childhood, and you did not have much fun so I can understand why you make certain decisions..." and on and on.

I knew when the devil was involved, so I prayed, "Lord hold my tongue, speak through me." When she was done I said, "First of all don't ever patronize me! Whatever you may be thinking, don't ever forget that I am still your mother. Second of all, you do not own a car, if something were to happen to the girls, I could not live with myself, because this trip is totally unnecessary. As for the other children, I did not give birth to them so they can do whatever they want. As grown as you think you are, you are still my responsibility, the bills still comes in my name, and the only home you have is mine. If my tone was harsh I apologize, but as for my position as your mother, I offer no apology. Now if you want to be like the other children, knock yourself out. If you want to do things without telling me, go right ahead. I know God did not tell you to share this with me, because when I got off the phone I asked Him to show me if I had taken the wrong approach in telling you not to involve other children in your plans, and He did not say anything differently so I suggest you go back to the Father, and do not allow the enemy to deceive you." She humbly said, "I don't want you to stop giving me your opinion; and you know that I will always listen to you and if you say I can't go I won't disobey you."

I just left it to God. That was last year 2004. She is now 20 and I have asked the Lord again, show me when to back off.

The opportunity came this January. One of her friends' has a time-share in Florida, and they even invited me along for spring break. I did not want to go. Sheri wanted to know if that meant she could not go. I told her whatever she and her Father decided, I would go along with it. I told her I would support her no matter what she decided. That was the hardest thing I had ever done in my life. Once again, they would be driving. She said, "Thanks, Mom," and we hung up. I prayed, "Lord, whatever you want her to do, I will go along with it. You know that I am not comfortable with the driving, but I trust your plan." A few weeks later the plan changed, now it was not Florida, it was Wisconsin. I gave the same answer, and got the same response, "Thanks, Mom." Again, I prayed, "Lord whatever you want, I will go along with it." She called me back later saying, she needed to update her passport for her study abroad program as it had expired. She would have to get it done over spring break, and there went the Wisconsin trip. When she realized this she said, "I am glad I am not going, I get to spend some time with you and we can do some things together." GOD IS GOOD AND FAITHFUL ALL THE TIME. Did I say she could not go? No, but I turned my cares over to our Father. Whatever He decides, I will go along with His plan.

Lesson number two. I had always gone to visit her at college unannounced. This year, I wanted to go for Valentines Day, but decided that spring break would be soon after and I did not want to make two trips that close together since the car was starting to rack up miles. But when Sheri told me that one of her friends would bring her home for spring break, which would save me a trip, I decided to go visit her for Valentine's Day as planned without letting her know. The big surprise weekend visit! We spoke that Wednesday night, and I still did not tell her of my plans. As we said goodnight, I suddenly felt the conviction of the Holy Spirit. I asked, "What's wrong? Do you want me to tell her?" No, He wanted me to *ask her permission* to go for a visit. What was happening? I had asked Him to teach me when it was time to back off and treat her like an adult; He was beginning the process. So I called my daughter back and the conversation went like this: "Sheri I have Friday off, is it ok for me to come for a visit?" There was a pause (I am sure it was shock even thought she played it cool). "Let me see what I have planned for Friday," was her response. I was as humble as a church mouse. She said, "Sure, mom." I said, "Are you sure it is ok?" "Yes Mommy. How long do you want to stay?" I told her I can stay until Sunday. It was all settled and the Holy Spirit gave me peace.

What happened there? The role was reversed. College was her territory, her space; I needed permission to visit. I baked her favorite cookies, and prepared for the visit. The Holy Spirit had given me rest again, because I had walked in obedience to His will. We had a great time that weekend. When we went out to dinner on Saturday night, I told her how new this whole letting go thing was to me, and that she would have to bear with me as I made the adjustment. She smiled as I told her about the surprise and how the Holy Sprit changed everything. She was appreciative of the Holy Spirit, (I take it the surprise would have been a real mistake). I told her I knew that I now had to get her permission to visit, and that it was hard making the transition. She told me she understood. We talked some more, affirmed our love and respect for each other and went back to her dorm. What a blessing that was. Change is never easy, but if we really trust God He will guide us through the time of transition.

BOY TALK

Long term communication matters

A word of caution before you read through this section; my approach may not work for everyone; it all depends on your lifestyle and home. God is as involved as you allow Him to be. I have observed that it is normal for young girls and boys to be encouraged to have "boyfriends/girlfriends" most times by their own parents. Some start as young as elementary school with the blessing of their parents. In most cases these children have not been told anything about sex or even life, and are left to experiment. Make-up begins much earlier making most young girls appear older than they really are, and their choice of clothing are even more frightening.

Sheridan was not allowed to wear nail polish or makeup until she was in high school and I took her for her first manicure. We talked about make-up and the joy of waiting. I told her she would have something to look forward to where most girls have already done it all. It was a wonderful experience for both of us. She was not allowed to have a boyfriend, as a matter of fact I told her not to even mention the subject before she was eighteen.

When I rededicated my life to the Lord, I made many requests for both of us, but especially for Sheridan. I prayed this prayer daily: "*Father I thank you that the wisdom of God and the mind of Christ is formed in her daily, I thank you that the excellent spirit of Daniel is formed in her, the integrity of Joseph is formed in her character, the servant's heart of obedience of Samuel be lived out in her and that the spirit of worship and praise of David be in her life always. I also thank you that you have already picked out her life mate, that she will not go from relationship to relationship, but that you guard her emotions as she waits on your choice, I thank you that he is a man of God, that he loves your word, your house and your people. I thank you that he is established in his career, and will be a good provider for her. I thank you that as she keeps herself pure, that he will also keep himself pure. I bless you Lord that she excels spiritually, academically, socially and in all areas of her life. She walks in divine health always, sickness and disease is far from her in Jesus name, her heart warms from your touch and her mind wanders to you always.* God has honored this time tested prayer. All that is missing is the mate, and I am not anxious. (Philippians 4:6-7)

Sheridan has many male friends, but no boyfriend. I have told her that friendship is less emotional and more freeing. Even if a particular relationship should develop, that at least they have established a friendship. That is priceless! She has often relayed to me, after observing a young woman crying over a broken relationship, "I was happy that wasn't me." Before we encourage our children to become seriously involved with the opposite sex, we need to teach them how to be friends. We also need to be sure that they are emotionally prepared for the possibility of a break up. All is *not* fair in love and war. Breaking up hurts, no matter how mature you are.

I have taught my daughter to enjoy her childhood, embrace the teenage years, and not to rush to grow up. Adulthood will last for the rest of her life, but childhood is but for a brief moment. She still wants to sit on my lap; we giggle like kids over silly things. Let your children be who they are--kids. I have taught Sheridan that she is a precious gift from God, and therefore not to be dated by just anyone. I have instructed her to not let young men speak to her in disrespectful ways, and she will discover that they have as much respect for her as she has for herself. I tell her to set her standards high, because she serves a God of excellence. She has been taught to never settle for less than the best from herself and others. She knows to never compromise her values for anything or anyone. I recall a very respectable young man asked Sheri to the senior prom at her school. I had instructed Sheri that if a young man came to pick her up and sat in his car blowing the horn that she should not leave with him. He should come to the door, ring the bell, address me first, and then ask for her. He should also open the door for her. I told her that if he got in the car and left her standing, she was to come back into the house. She is a lady, and should be treated as nothing less. So, on prom night I waited to see what would happen. Well, he came to the door, we had a nice chat, then she came down the stairs and his eyes just lit up. I watched for the look, lust or respect, and it was total respect. As they left, he opened the door for her, held her wrap, made sure she was in and closed the door. Because this was not an exclusive date, they spent time with all of their friends. They didn't have to spend all evening with each other, and they had a great time. Today they are the best of friends. I have driven her to the shore to visit with him, he has come to our home, they have gone out to dinner as friends, and the respect is still there.

Parents, take the pressure off! Some young men as well as young women are ridiculed by their parents for not being interested in dating, and are even accused of being "gay." Let God lead them. In His time, He will bring them into healthy relationships. Stop the name-calling and the put-downs. I have never spoken down to Sheri, never called her stupid, or blamed her for my failures. She does not have a "significant other" because it is just not God's time, not because something is wrong with her. I would prefer for her to remain unattached than to see her go from one relationship to another. Teach your children to let God choose their friends as well as marriage partners. That is exactly what I did. That is why I started by saying this may not be for everyone. I guess I am weird too; I have not dated since she was 2 and one-half years old. My motto has always been "the right one is worth the wait." I would really prefer God's choice over my own or hers. Single parents, do not allow your desires for companionship to scar your sons and daughters. There have been countless times when mothers have ignored the signs of sexual or physical abuse against their children by their boyfriends because of their own need for companionship. Never sell your children for what is temporal! Remember, they will imitate the worst in us as well as the best in us. No relationship, no matter how wonderful, other than the one you share with Jesus, is more valuable than the one you share with your children as a single parent. **But my God shall supply all my needs according to His riches in glory by Christ Jesus**. Philippians 4:19. **ALL!** That word implies a mate, emotional needs and desires, food, shelter, clothing and finances. Do not allow neediness, be it emotional or financial to control your decisions. We are not alone when our trust is in Him.

In her first year of college, Sheri introduced me to a Christian young man. I saw right away that she liked him and he liked her but I could also see that he liked her as a friend, and Sheri liked him a little more. I waited until we were driving home about 3 months after the introduction, because I needed time to pray about it first, to approach the subject. I had told the Lord that if this was all right, that it was fine with me too. I said "You really like this boy, don't you?" She responded, "yes" as I expected. I continued, "Sometimes we can really like someone, but the problem is, even though the person may like us, it may not be at the same level. I continued saying you showed me the valentine's card he wrote you. I noticed that he ended it by saying that he was so blessed that you were his sister in the Lord, and how much he respected your faith walk. That leads me to believe that he is not thinking about a serious relationship. Do not allow yourself to expect more than he is prepared to give to the friendship. Enjoy what you have, and if it is your Father's plan, it will all work itself out. She was so thankful for our talk. I was grateful that God showed up again to protect her emotions.

Another time we were at lunch off campus and she asked, "Mommy what kind of young man would you approve of me dating?" I told her that he had to be born again, filled with the Holy Spirit, he had to love the Lord, because if he did not then she would be unequally yoked (2 Corinthians 6:14-16). I told her that if he loved the Lord, he would respect her. I heard a well known preacher say something I never forgot. He told his congregation that if someone shows up for your daughter and you do not approve, do not allow your daughter to leave with him. He said when his daughter asked if the person at the door was for her, he said "No! He is not for you!" When Sheri was a young teen I said to her, "If you bring a young man home and I say to you, he is not for you, do not get angry, I have already asked the Holy Spirit about him, if he says no, go along with Him." I remind her often to pray about everything and trust God's responses. I taught her not to question His silence or responses. If He is in control, trust His heart. I have also told my daughter, if a young man shows interest in her, before she makes a decision, tell him he will have to meet me. If he resists or complains, she is to let him go immediately. I want to know who he is.

STAYING INVOLVED

On a different note, when Sheri was in the 11th grade, she got a job as a babysitter. Someone at the summer camp where she worked recommended her to a couple that had two children. When the interested family called to speak with Sheri, I had her tell them that I would like to meet with them at their home before she took the job. When we went over, they remarked that they knew they were getting a responsible person, because I was the first parent to ever make such a request. I was shocked and responded, "God has given me a responsibility to look out for her well being. She is my only child. I need to know about you, your home, your expectations, the ages of the children, special needs etc. I know she is seventeen, but I take nothing for granted. You are married, so I also wanted to meet your husband," and I interviewed them. No money is worth my child's safety. I dropped her off and picked her up, for a while because sometimes it was very late when the couple returned home. Sheridan was a new driver so I would ask the Lord to let me know when it was time to let her make the 45 minute drive alone. Soon He allowed me to let her drive there with me in the car, then when I went to get her, let her drive home. The time would soon come for her to go it alone, at which point she would call as soon as she got there, and when she was about to leave, I could always time her. She had proven to be responsible. Age does not determine maturity. Get to know your children. Do not allow society to determine their readiness. God will always let you know when the time is right for the next important stage of your child's development. My daughter has been driving for at least three years now, and she has started a new job during her summer and winter breaks. I am sometimes on vacation while she's at work. Her job is located in the city of Newark, which is a new driving area for her. I had her drive to work with me in the car, and had planned to have her drive home, just to familiarize her with the traffic patterns. On my way to pick her up having planned in advance to have her drive home that evening, the Holy Spirit said "Not today." At first I questioned whether it was my apprehension, but He was very persistent. When I pulled up at her office she got into the car and said, "You don't have a peace about me driving home, right?" I told her what happened and she responded I figured as much. The next day as I went to pick her up I had this awesome sense of peace about letting her drive home. What was the difference? I do not know what God had us avoid the day before, but my obedience may have saved both our lives. If He is Lord of all, He has the right to change even our best plans for our children—even when *we* think they're ready.

CHAPTER 12

DISOBEDIENCE STILL HAS ITS CONSEQUENCES

Even though I had done everything the Lord instructed me relative to raising my daughter, the one thing I was not prepared for was what happened one Wednesday night while we were having some down time together watching Everybody Loves Raymond and dining on fine Italian food. Out of the blue, I began to share how God had been using my six years of memories with my dad prior to his death to draw me closer to Him. I was just sharing how my love for Dad had strengthened my fellowship with the Father and that I had no clue why God was using that at this time. All of a sudden my daughter began sharing how she'd been feeling since the age of eighteen that she could not say 'Father' anymore in reference to the Lord, but simply "God." She felt that because she did not have the experience of having an earthly father, she was having a harder time relating to God as a father.

This revelation was not only shocking, but disturbing because right away I sensed the enemy capitalizing on the situation. I also knew why God had me bring this subject up in the first place. He would not let her leave the country for a semester of study abroad with that gaping hole in her emotions. Why He had said nothing to me up to that point was not known, but it was obvious that He wanted it dealt with. We turned off the television and I began telling her the following:

"If you are looking for someone to blame please, blame me. I am the one who walked in disobedience. Sin will always carry consequences, but please do not ruin your relationship with your Heavenly Father because of what I did."

The Holy Spirit guided me through this very delicate situation, and I asked my daughter to tell her Father God that she loved Him. I said, "Call Him 'Father', Sheri." She could not. I kept at it until she began to weep. I prayed with her, and let her cry. After she stopped crying, I repeated the request. I knew this had to be done or the enemy would use this as a stronghold. When she finally repeated the words, we could both sense the enemy's defeat and her victory. I asked if she wanted to get in touch with her biological father, and she said no, so I left it alone. I shared some scriptures with her, we prayed, and we hugged. The Holy Spirit continued to minister and heal as we worshipped and praised God for interrupting our evening. We thanked Him for using what He was doing in me to reveal what was going on in Sheri's heart and for bringing release.

Sin is always a reproach, but I thank God for His righteousness. Satan may have had a couple of years of bondage, but Jehovah got the glory. I close by saying sensitivity is of the utmost importance. What transpired did not come about because we were in prayer but when you make God a priority, He has the freedom to break in at any time. My willingness to cooperate saved my daughter's emotional, spiritual, and physical life. I never would have known, but for Him. To God, be the glory!

At this time I would like to add a word of caution to parents who become born again when their children are teen-agers. Whatever changes you may see the need to make in your home, please do so gradually all the while seeking the heart of God. You will definitely need His wisdom. Your children, most likely have been accustomed to life without Christian values, if you begin to make what to them may seem like legalistic changes you are in for the greatest challenges of your life.

Now that your spiritual eyes have been opened to see all the things you may have been doing wrong your instinct IS SHOUTING CHARGE! But just hold your horses. Approach these desires with caution. Allow the Lord to show you how to proceed. Remember the Devil is not too pleased with your decision for Christ. He will do whatever it takes to disrupt your home and lives. I recall giving these same instructions to a single mom of a teenage daughter. I admonished her to speak with her daughter openly of her decision to follow Christ. I encouraged her to apologize for the things she had allowed her to do because of a lack of godly wisdom. When someone has not had food for a long period of time, we never introduce steak and potatoes into their diet, we generally begin with a light broth or some form of liquid, and this is done over time until the individual is strong enough to eat "solid food." This is no different when you are starting to change years of old behavior patterns that, to your teenager was alright for over 14 or 16 years. I told her to introduce changes gradually and honestly, not to abruptly stop her from doing the things once allowed, but communicate to her why there were going to be changes because of the principles in the Word of God. Explain that these changes are not intended to hurt or control but rather to protect and free her from situations that will eventually bring harm. Just trust God.

She did not heed my advice, but did the complete opposite of what I had said. Her decision resulted in aggressive rebellion. The child begun to lie and sneak around, eventually she became pregnant and now has two children outside of marriage. We cannot change things overnight. God in His wisdom has taken His time in shaping us. We are instructed to daily "renew our minds" (Romans 12:2) why? Because the old nature is hard to control, in one clean sweep. We work at the change that has taken place in our hearts. As we live what we say, they will be won to by our lives. Honest communication will go a long way in stemming rebellion. Trust in the Lord, He has given us the promise of salvation to our whole house. (Acts 2:39; 16:31)

CHAPTER 13

IT'S NEVER OVER

When does parenting end? NEVER! When does the concern stop? NEVER! We will always be parents. I am more confident today that I have done a God job than I have ever been, now that she has left the teenage years to embark on the twenties. She is more committed to her faith now than ever before. She has declared her major in college, will be studying abroad in her junior year, and I can't wait to see what the next move of our Father will be. We have invited Him along for the duration of our earthly lives, and we wait in anticipation for His daily unveilings. As we trust Him He promises never to leave or forsake us. Whose life is it anyway? If you have given your children to Him, then trust Him to teach you how to raise them His way.

I pray this book will be a blessing to all who read it. I have no citations except the scriptures. I have shared my own personal experiences, as the Spirit of God has led. As parents, our first priority is to our God and our families. If He is not Lord of all He is not Lord at all. All I have is praise and thanksgiving for Him. When He first gave me the dream of writing, I said Lord, who am I? There are parents who have raised good, Godly children, what makes my experiences any different? Only He knows. Sheridan took me to Barnes and Nobles and told me to walk around and visualize my books on the shelves. Since the dream, whenever we go to a bookstore, unbeknownst to me, she would be doing the same. She has been my inspiration. She more than anyone can substantiate the claims of this book because, it is her life, and she continues to live it. This book and the others will be dedicated to my Lord and Savior because without Him I would have no dream. This is His book, may He do with it what brings Him glory and honor.

(Genesis 17:1-2) GOD'S PROMISE TO ME 1/6/03

FINAL THOUGHTS
By Sheridan Tennant

☙

Well, I am sure after reading all of this you must be wondering whether or not I can verify all that has been disclosed in these pages. I promise you, it's all true— I was editor number one. Growing up without a father or brothers and sisters can be a challenge.

Growing up God's way with a mother that sought the Lord every morning and night for you, fought for you, cried over you, admonished you when you needed it, and when you hadn't even done anything, makes a HUGE difference. I wouldn't have wanted it any other way. Now, I know you must also be thinking, you're not a normal child, or some may say I am just another super compliant child. Well, I can assure you, I am not. I have made mistakes, I have done some pretty stupid things like any other kid, and I received my share of punishments. But what has made all the difference has been my relationship with God. I cannot do anything without thinking about His perspective. I cannot go anywhere without wondering if my Heavenly Father approves—and of course, what would mommy think?

Now, I will admit, when I was a child I found her child-rearing techniques strange, sometimes harsh and old-fashioned, and I sometimes wondered how I could have ever been this woman's daughter, because we are very, very different people. But now, as a young woman, I THANK GOD, because He knew exactly what He was doing. Looking back over my child-hood however deprived or strict you may have thought it to be, I would not change a thing.

I have learned a lot from watching my Mommy. She is bold, she is hard-working, she is strong, but most of all, she LOVES the Lord with all of her heart and soul—and that is what I admire most. We have had some very difficult times. I've had my share of crying myself to sleep wondering where the money we needed for things would come from. I've had to be the strong one sometimes, praying over her, encouraging her when bills far exceeded her income. I've had my doubts, fears, frustrations and questions. But despite the hardships, God has remained faithful, and I don't know where I would be without Him.

At this time, I wanted to share with you just how significant being raised God's way has been to me—specifically in the area of growing up without a father. From the time I was born until this very day, my mother has prayed over my emotions, asking God to never let me feel slighted, or worthless because I did not have a father present in my life. She never wanted me to feel that void, she did not want me to follow the path of the statistically fatherless girls, which were often drug- addicted, teen mothers and desperate for any man they could get. That was not the life she wanted for me, and she asked God to shield me. And He did. Sitting here, I cannot think of a time growing up when I ever felt the burning need for an earthly father, or ever experienced pain or anger at not having him around. God completely cushioned me during my sensitive, formative years. He keeps His promises. But when I turned 18, things changed for me.

I had always been raised to call God 'Father.' In prayer it was always, "Father God" or simply, "Father, in the name of Jesus..." But the Father portion was always there, because that's what I knew, and that's what He was to me. But in my later teenage years that void that I had never felt became exposed. It was as if God stepped out, and allowed me to feel just a little of what He had been sparing me from. His intention, as I understand it now, was to help me to draw closer to Him and truly, for the first time, acknowledge Him as Father, and more specifically, Daddy God. During this very uncomfortable transition, my mother had conveniently chosen to calling God "Daddy" all the time. It frustrated, annoyed and even infuriated me. Daddy? Who was that? *What* was that? How could she call someone she had never seen something so personal? I knew I couldn't, and from that moment on, a wall began to form.

As I passed through the ages of 18 to 20, this wall continued to get stronger. Soon I was neglecting my personal worship time with God, I had the hardest time saying "Father," and my mother's "Daddy Gods'" were driving me insane. Instead of drawing closer to my Father, I was pushing Him away, under the misconception that, "Well, I never had a Father, so it's just harder for me to see God that way, so He'll just have to accept that." Meanwhile, my desire for a boyfriend, or male attention, was increasing. Any boy that showed me attention would completely enrapture my attention and I would mentally plan our wedding over just a few kind words exchanged. I wanted someone to love me. I wanted someone (other than mommy) to hold me and tell me that I was the most important girl in the world to them. I wanted someone to protect me and listen when I had a problem and comfort me.....a Father. But, I didn't see that, until one evening when I was home for the summer my mother began talking to me about how precious her time with "Daddy God" had been recently. I was listening, but not really. I was sick of the Daddy reference and I was just ready to tune it all out when she or the Holy Ghost began to hit some nerves. I found myself pouring out every thought I'd had for the last three years about how hard it was to see God as a Father anymore and how this void was open and I didn't understand what was happening. I was bitter, and I was building a separation between me and God and I knew it, but didn't know how to fix it. My mother said to me, "Sheri, call him father." I sat there dumfounded. She repeated, "Sheridan, say it. Say, 'Father'." I couldn't do it. Within minutes, I was sobbing like I had never sobbed before and all of the years of questions, pain, frustration and bitterness about being "fatherless" came pouring out of me. My mother let me cry and she prayed over my bowed head as I sobbed on her lap. Then she said, "Sheri, say 'I love you, Father'." It took several moments, and the first few times just a whisper could emerge, but through the struggle, I said it, and I was instantly freed of the burden I had been carrying for three years. She took the time to explain how the enemy had set out to cause a rift in my relationship with my Father. That the void that I felt at 18 was not for a "missing male" but it was God's way of drawing me closer to Himself.

What if my mother was not sensitive to the Holy Spirit? What if my mother had not raised me to love the Lord, and to see Him as my Father? What if she had chosen to raise me as she had been raised, with religion, harsh unfeeling discipline, and no love or affection? I would have become just like every other fatherless girl. But praise be to God, my *Father*, that in His infinite mercy He saved us both, and gave my mother the wisdom to live for Him, and raise me with Him. He is the only Father I have and need. The devil has always wanted to side track me, and this was a very tender and vulnerable spot for me. But he was exposed.

So, in conclusion to all that you have read about raising your children God's way, I just wanted you to hear from me that it has not been easy. And as you can see from this little bit I've shared with you, there are plenty of tears involved. But I thank God for every lesson learned. I am 20 years old, and I still need my Mommy. I still come to her for advice, prayer, counsel and wisdom. She is still parenting me. Yes, I am a woman now, and I make a lot of decisions on my own, but, I always include my parents-God my Father and Mommy. You can never go wrong following God's lead. Please don't make the mistake of thinking you can raise your children all by yourself. I only hope and pray that when my day comes to be a Mom, I have half the wisdom and fore-sight that my mother has. But guess what? I can! Because the same Jesus that resides in her, that gave her all of the wisdom that she had in raising me, lives in me,. What a legacy and a prize! Why would you want your children to have anything less than God's best? Do yourself, and them, a favor—raise them God's way. I am living proof that it works.

Endorsements

"A Single Parent's Guide to Raising Children God's Way" is insightful and offers valuable "life lessons" to any parent (single or married) raising a child in today's society. Unfortunately, our schools, the media and their peers have been the model for the values, morals and standards set for our children instead of the commandments given to us by God, our Father, who created us. Winsome Tennant shares personal and often heartfelt experiences that can touch even the most resistant child. If you are struggling with any challenges in regards to nurturing Godly children, you will most assuredly find this book to be rewarding and beneficial in raising a child that will love and respect you and most importantly love the Lord.

Eugene Brown
Principal
Newark Public Schools/
Praise and Worship Orchestra Director @ Faith Fellowship
Ministries World Outreach Center, Sayreville, New Jersey

As an avid reader I have found "A Single Parent's Guide to Raising Children God's Way, to be a religious book with principles that may be applied in a secular world. It is instructive and informative, some parts made me laugh others made me cry but all of made me pray. Miss Tennant has the ability to capture your attention, hold it and do a dance in it; I read 126 pages in one sitting! I was employed by a police department for 13 years and have raised three wonderful children and I tell you I have NEVER seen the things I see today. I am shocked by the hate crimes and brutality that is caused by our children. We have been told by society what we are allowed to do in the area of discipline and child rearing, but who is giving positive advice, telling us tried and true methods that work in this extremely frustrating time? Winsome Tennant is. She lives what she has written. I have known her and her daughter for quite some time and I can attest to the fact that Miss Tennant, although a single parent who has come from an extremely abusive background, has broken the cycle of abuse and used the principles in her book to raise a beautiful, God centered, well rounded young lady. This book will bless you!

Reverend Christine Ritter-Harris
Senior Pastor, Citadel of Hope Worship Center
Montclair, New Jersey

I wish I had this book 30 years ago when I was raising my child.

Dianne C. Marus
Chief Financial Officer, Township of Montclair

I have had the distinct pleasure of knowing Winsome Tennant for over 25 years. We have been very good friends and have at times attended the same church and been neighbors. Winsome has worked through difficult circumstances with commitment and faith and a consistent positive outlook. Winsome has raised her daughter totally by herself, all the while walking with God. She has been very successful in raising her daughter to be a good person, a woman of faith and an outstanding student. I watched her work as a parent and at times thought she was too strict, but I have been proven wrong. I am delighted to see the success of her parenting approach, which I know is rooted in faith. The book is an out-growth of both their lives and will prove to be a blessing to all who read it.

Barbara Nagle, JD
Associate Professor of Legal Studies
Montclair State University, Montclair New Jersey

Single parent or two parent family, it does not matter the principles are timely and beneficial to anyone raising children today. Whether you are married or single, if you are planning on having children this book will prove to be a blessing to you.

Delroy Tennant
Brother of Author

Printed in the United States
60387LVS00001BB/1-102